WAI
THE GALL

Craigwhannel is climbed via an unplanted swathe. (Walk 21)

WALKING THE GALLOWAY HILLS

by

Paddy Dillon

CICERONE PRESS
MILNTHORPE, CUMBRIA

Reprinted 2003
1 85284 168 0
A catalogue record for this book is available from the British Library.

ADVICE TO READERS

Readers are advised that whilst every effort is taken by the author to ensure the accuracy of this guidebook, changes can occur which may affect the contents. A book of this nature with detailed descriptions and detailed maps is more prone to change than a more general guide. New fences and stiles appear, waymarking alters, there may be new buildings or eradication of old buildings. It is advisable to check locally on transport, accommodation, shops etc. Even rights of way can be altered, paths can be eradicated by landslip, forest clearances or changes of ownership. The publisher would welcome notes of any such changes.

Other Cicerone books by the same author:
The Mountains of Ireland
Walking in the North Pennines

Front Cover: Curleywee as seen from Buchan Burn. (Walk 5)

CONTENTS

LONGER WALKS

Introduction

"BE WARNED,
IT'S GOING TO BE TOUGH UNDERFOOT THIS YEAR"

The Galloway Hills are the highlands of south-west Scotland - a tract of rocky, boggy, wilderness hills with some forest cover. Much of the area has been designated as the Galloway Forest Park, offering almost unlimited access for walkers. One guidebook calls the Galloway Hills "A Walker's Paradise". The quote at the top of the page, however, is taken from publicity for the 1986 Karrimor International Mountain Marathon, which was held in the Galloway Hills. The statement can be amended slightly for walkers using this guidebook - "Be warned, it's going to be tough underfoot *every* year!" Although this guide includes a couple of easy forest trails, many more of the routes head for the hills where paths are few and the ground is exceptionally rugged. Extracts from the detailed Harveys Walker's Map of the Galloway Hills illustrate 33 day walks, then brief notes describe seven longer walks. You can marvel at the wilderness qualities of the hills, or follow the wanderings of Robert the Bruce, or base yourself at a remote bothy to enjoy walks in the heart of the Galloway Hills. With virtual freedom to roam in any direction the Galloway Hills are truly a walker's paradise, but remember that paradise is a difficult condition to attain and is generally associated with a path of suffering too!

THE BARE BONES

There are four rugged ranges of hills in this guide - the Range of the Awful Hand, the Rhinns of Kells, the Minnigaff Hills and the Dungeon Hills. The oldest rocks occur around the edge of the area, being represented by Ordovician strata which were laid down around 500 million years ago. The Loch Doon Granite forms most of the hill groups and this arrived later in a molten mass which was squeezed into the Earth's crust under immense pressure during a period of mountain building. This mass melted some of the older Ordovician rocks, or at least baked them in intense heat so that their mineral structures were altered - a process called metamorphism.

Those far-off days of mountain building are long past, and the present-day shape of the hills is due to a quite different process. A mere million years ago the land was gripped in an Ice Age, a period which ended only 10,000 years ago, which is nothing on a geological timescale. As vast accumulations of snow and ice built up over the original Galloway Hills, the pressure and weight of the ice caused it to "flow" downslope as glaciers. The ice moved slowly, but inexorably, grinding broken rock against rockfaces as it travelled, carving bowl-shaped corries out of the high hills and deepening the valleys to leave them with steep sides and level floors. All we see today are the shapes of ice-scoured rock and the masses of low-lying glacial rubble, or moraine, which was transported within the ice.

A GLIMPSE OF HISTORY

Scotland's colourful and turbulent history is well represented around the fringes of the Galloway Hills, but seldom did anything of note occur within their bleak confines. The first hunter-gatherers settled along the coastal margins so that they could live off the produce of both the land and the sea. The hills will have been clothed in their original wildwoods, with swampy areas and wild beasts. Although a horde of Bronze Age implements was found on the Fell of Eschoncan, there are no traces of any hill forts or permanent settlements. There is, however, a reconstructed Romano-British house near Clatteringshaws Loch. Although Whithorn and Galloway are associated with the dawning of Christianity in Scotland, all the old churches and big abbeys are located some distance from the hills.

We're well into historical times before there are truly momentous happenings on the hills. Robert the Bruce and his tiny army of a few hundred were hemmed into these wild hills by thousands of English troops. The Bruce had killed Red Comyn and hastily assumed kingship. Despite early successes he was later forced to flee for his life, then had difficulty raising an army. He embarked on a campaign of guerrilla warfare from the hills, where he used the rocky, boggy terrain to his advantage in 1307. With each success he was able to demoralise the enemy and increase his own support, until he was able to break from the hills and extend his campaign throughout Scotland, finally thrashing the English at Bannockburn in 1314.

In the turbulent years of the "Killing Times" through the latter half of the 1600s, the hills again provided a refuge and safe haven for people fleeing religious persecution. Furious debates had centred on the need for bishops in the Scottish church, and the extent of authority the king should wield. Fiery preachers sprang up and some clerics were ousted from their parishes, and as dissent was punishable by heavy fines, imprisonment, torture or death, secret "conventicles" were held in the hills. Even so, some people were killed while attending these prayer meetings in the hills and there are monuments to the "Covenanters" all over Galloway. There's a story behind every monument and the victims are widely regarded as martyrs.

A novel called *The Raiders* by S.R.Crockett again focuses our attention on the hills. Although fact and fiction are woven together in the story, these hills really were used as a hideaway for fierce gypsy clans - notably the Faas, Marshalls and Macatericks. They seem to have lived by raiding cattle and stealing goods from their neighbours. The most colourful character in those times was surely Billy Marshall, widely regarded as the gypsy "king". He is reputed to have lived for 120 years, dying in 1792. Many stories are told about him throughout the region and they surely contain at least a grain of truth.

The few farms that ever managed to eke an existence out of the wild interior of the Galloway Hills were abandoned and falling ruinous by 1900. The land came into the hands of the Forestry Commission and sheep rearing was replaced by timber growing. The planting started in 1922, so some stands are coming into maturity and are being clear-felled. Replanting is taking place so that timber can be harvested in the future.

THE GALLOWAY FOREST PARK

The Galloway Forest Park covers much of the Forestry Commission's holdings in the Galloway Hills. Some 250 square miles (670sq km) of land was designated as a Forest Park in 1943. Although the Forestry Commission's primary purpose is to produce timber, not all the land has been planted. There are no plantations on the highest hills, where the trees simply do not thrive, nor have all the boggy valleys been planted, even though they would support forest cover.

The needs of conservation and recreation have been recognised and the Forestry Commission have provided some basic amenities and interpretative facilities for visitors, as well as allowing virtual free access on foot. A number of leaflets have been prepared which cover forest trails and other points of interest.

FLORA AND FAUNA

Throughout this guide, only the most basic flora is mentioned, particularly in relation to walking conditions. Heather is widespread, but nowhere does it form the uniform cover typical of moorlands which are "managed" for grouse-shooting. It generally indicates fairly dry ground and can occur on even quite rocky ground with patches of bilberry. Scree slopes, however, are too dry for anything but specialist plants such as parsley fern. The highest summits are usually covered in short, green grass which is a delight to walk across, but by contrast the boggy valleys support only the wiry moor grasses which raise themselves in tussocks above the waterlogged peaty soils. You'll often find these boggy valleys brightened by nodding heads of cotton grass or yellow bog asphodel. Bog myrtle is an aromatic shrub which is seldom more than knee high. It has a special liking for wet ground and cannot survive if a drainage ditch is cut close to its roots. Whenever standing water occurs you may find bright green sphagnum moss developing. This moss is like a sponge, so you should chart a course round any patches you see to avoid wet feet. Only a few remnants of the original forest cover survive, notably the patchy oakwoods of Glen Trool. A few hardy rowans cling to rocky faces away from herbivores, but any Scots pine you see are likely to be secondary plantings. The current forest cover is made up of imported species with sitka spruce dominating. Visit the Tree Plots near Stroan House in Glen Trool to familiarise yourself with the various species.

The most magnificent animal to be seen in the Galloway Hills is the red deer, though shy roe deer are also present. There are large herds of "wild" goats with impressive sweeping horns and shaggy coats. The local breed of cattle is the distinctive "belted" Galloway, though you may notice a few Highland too. Visit the Palgowan Open Farm to find out more. Foxes and hares run even to the highest summits, while the woodlands still support red squirrels. Otters

Adders are found in the Galloway Hills

may occasionally be noticed in the watercourses, while fishermen come in search of brown trout, salmon and even pike. You may catch a glimpse of a common lizard basking in the sun, or even find adders in some places. Although adders are poisonous, they have no great wish to meet people and are more content catching small rodents, frogs and insects.

Insect life is dominated - at least in the minds of summer visitors - by the midge! Mosquito larvae develop in almost any pool of standing water and rise on the wing as adults. The males form clouds where they hover and whine for female mates. The females, having mated, develop a blood-lust which must be satisfied before they can lay their eggs - and that's where you come in! The eggs are laid in pools of water and so the cycle goes on and on. Rain, wind or strong sun generally keep the midges down, otherwise you may have to use a repellent. There are species of butterflies on the moorlands, as well as the day-flying emperor moth and amazing metallic-hued dragonflies.

Mixed woodlands support many species of bird, including pied flycatchers where there are sufficient nesting holes, green woodpeckers even this far west, chiffchaff, wood warblers and flocks of chaffinches wherever there are picnic crumbs to be had. Although young forest plantations offer good cover for many species of bird, mature stands have no undergrowth and little food, so they can be eerily silent places. Crossbills, of course, have specially adapted beaks for picking at pine cones, so they can be noticed as visitors. Dippers and grey wagtails frequent the watercourses, while the lochs attract various species of duck, geese and waterfowl. You may occasionally find a raucous colony of black-headed gulls deserting the sea and occupying a lonely moorland pool. The moors are sometimes noisy with the calls of lapwing, curlew and grouse, but look out for snipe, dunlin, golden plover and greenshank too. Ravens can usually be seen circling rocky fastnesses, while birds of prey include hen harrier, kestrel, sparrowhawk and an occasional eagle. The sheer variety of wildlife habitats and the proximity of the sea means that almost anything could be spotted either in residence or migrating.

ACCESS AND ACCOMMODATION

Public transport barely touches the Galloway Hills. If you were arriving by train you'd have to link with the Girvan to Newton Stewart bus at Barrhill, which will take you to Glentrool Village - and that's your lot! Motorists have access to Glen Trool, as well as having car parks along the Straiton road, Carrick Forest Drive and off the Queen's Road, as well as the use of access roads to Craigencallie or Auchinleck. Beyond all these points you have to walk. "You are welcome to walk anywhere in the Park" is the way one leaflet puts it, which is handy as there are so few trodden paths. You have to remember that this free access carries responsibilities. You must not damage any trees, so use forest roads and rides on your walks, and never cut down a tree for fuel. Firewood is provided near most of the bothies. Do not light fires in the open as they can get out of control on the moors or beside trees and can cause extensive damage. Access can be temporarily restricted for safety reasons when clear-felling and timber extraction is being carried out.

There are no lodgings to be had in the wilds except for the bothies at Culsharg, Tunskeen, Backhill of Bush and White Laggan. These offer basic shelter and the option of a log fire, and they must be left in good order for the next occupants. You can't guarantee space in a bothy, so you might like to carry a tent as insurance. There are campsites at Caldons and Talnotry which are both operated by the Forestry Commission. There seems to be no great objection to tents being pitched for a night or two in the more remote parts of the hills, but you shouldn't establish long-term camps and should always leave your pitch spotlessly clean. The nearest youth hostels are at Minnigaff and Kendoon, with scout huts available at Mid Garrary and Castlemaddy. A range of hotels and B&Bs can be found in and around Newton Stewart, with lodgings also offered at New Galloway, Dalry, Carsphairn, Dalmellington and Bargrennan. Full details can be obtained from Tourist Information Centres.

FAMILIARISATION WITH THE AREA

Motorists can become familiar with the range of facilities around the Galloway Hills on a simple day tour which is conveniently started at Newton Stewart. Follow the Queen's Road (A712) towards New Galloway, noting the campsite at Talnotry, Murray's Monument, Wild Goat Park and Red Deer Range. You can drive along the access road to Craigencallie, then return to have a look at the Clatteringshaws Forest Wildlife Centre, or Deer Museum. Continue to New Galloway, which is Scotland's smallest burgh, then follow the A713 to Dalry and The Glenkens. Note that you have access to Forrest Lodge for walks in the Rhinns of Kells, though you must return to the main road. Carsphairn is a lovely little village with a few heritage trails, while Polmaddie has further access to the Rhinns of Kells.

Continue as if for Dalmellington, but follow the Loch Doon road and have a look at Loch Doon Castle. The Carrick Forest Drive comes next, and you can pick up a ticket from a "pay and display" machine. At the end of the Forest Drive a minor road runs to Stinchar Bridge where you turn left along the Glentrool Village road. You can check out the number of car parks along this road, especially the one at Kirriereoch. You could also visit Palgowan Open Farm. Drive the length of Glen Trool and have a look at the visitor centre, Caldons Campsite and the Bruce's Stone. Return through the glen and head for Bargrennan and the A714 to reach Newton Stewart and its excellent range of services. If you've still a few minutes to spare you could check out the access road to Auchinleck. After this tour you'll be aware of all the main parking places and access roads, as well as the range of facilities close to the hills. All the walks described in this guide lie within the circuit you've driven around.

THOSE CRAZY NAMES

The map of the Galloway Hills is peppered with placenames which look as if they've been designed by a committee of linguists at loggerheads. Maybe that's not too far from the truth. The oldest language used in the area was Gaelic, with some mixing of Scottish and Irish variations throughout the centuries. There may have been some infiltration of the later Brythonic, Welsh-type language from Cumbria. Norse invaders brought a new language pattern, as did the Norman/English with their Old French. As English developed as a language it was brought into contact with the developing Scots tongue, with all the dialect variations in both tongues. If you're prepared to dig deep into the placenames of the Galloway Hills you'll find all sorts of languages buried there, but at the end of the day they're all describing quite ordinary landscape features.

Curleywee, for instance, has its roots in the Gaelic *Cor na Gaeth,* which means Hill of the Wind. Neighbouring Millfore may be derived from the Gaelic *Mull Fhuar,* or Cold Hill. The rig, clint, fell and holm placenames are all Norse in origin. Some names have become so corrupted that their meaning can only be guessed at. The best thing you can do is to accept the placenames at their face value and relish their noble and dramatic sounds: The Rhinns of Kells, Rig of the Jarkness, Nieve of the Spit, Shalloch on Minnoch, Clints of the Buss, Buckdas of Cairnbaber, Point of the Snibe, Mullwharchar, Craigeazle, and many others to stir your imagination and inspire you to poetry!

THE WALKS

The walks in this guide include a couple of short, easy, waymarked forest trails. These are the exception, though some of the other walks aren't too difficult. However, many of the walks head for the hills, and there is plenty of boggy, rocky ground up there. Paths are few and far between, though some of the approach routes use clear, firm, broad forest roads. You need to exercise great care when walking across pathless boggy ground, or tussocky moorlands where you could turn an ankle, as well as when crossing steep, rocky slopes. You also need to be very careful after heavy rain swells the river, particularly the dark, deep, dangerous "lanes" which need to be forded on some of the walks. Wherever possible, bridges are used, but in some cases you simply have no choice but to ford at some shallow point. When the rivers are in spate, therefore, some of the walks simply can't be completed. All 33 of the day walks are circular and none of them stands in complete isolation. All the walks can be linked with one or two other walks, so that you have plenty of information to enable you to alter the routes if required, or to amass details which enable you to complete much longer expeditions through the hills. In broad outline, the walks start in Glen Trool and work their way through the Range of the Awful Hand, then across to the Rhinns of Kells, through the Minnigaff Hills to return to Glen Trool, then some very rugged walks into the Dungeon Hills are described. Brief details are offered of seven longer walks which you might consider if you've the energy and ability to complete them, but these are more difficult. Most of the day walks start from a car park, but to avoid lengthy walk-ins a number of routes are suggested which assume you'll be using one of the bothies as a base for your explorations.

THE MAPS

The maps in this guide which illustrate the 33 day walks are extracted from the Harveys Walker's Map of the Galloway Hills. This is the best and most detailed map of the area for walkers. It shows landscape details which include such essential features as boggy and rocky ground, forest rides and trodden paths - even odd cairns and boulders in some places. The map doesn't show non-essential items such as local government boundaries, but it does show walls and fences which you can use as guides in poor visibility. The grid system is exactly the same as that used on Ordnance Survey maps, while the scale is a generous 1:40,000. The extracts in this guide are printed in monochrome with the route shown in colour. It's highly recommended that you use this guide in conjunction with the Harveys map, which is printed in full colour on a tough, fully waterproof paper, as well as being supplied in a clear plastic cover with a visitor guide.

The Galloway Hills map, like others in the Harveys series, was produced for the Karrimor International Mountain Marathon, but continues to be updated regularly. The Karrimor has been held twice in the Galloway Hills and both times has suffered from appalling weather and there's been a staggering retirement rate in excess of 50%. Many upland areas have hosted the Karrimor event and so have been mapped by Harveys. Coverage includes areas as far apart as the Cairngorms and Dartmoor, with popular mountainous areas mapped such as Snowdonia, the English Lake District and the Trossachs. Full details of titles available can be obtained from Harveys, 12-16 Main Street, Doune, Perthshire FK16 6BJ, or telephone (01786) 841202. The relevant Ordnance Survey Landranger map covering the same area is number 77 and the Pathfinder series also covers the area in several sheets, but without the same detailed coverage of the Harveys map.

TOURIST INFORMATION

For accommodation details, maps and supporting publications, or details of opening times of visitor centres, the main Tourist Information Centre for the area is at Dashwood Square in Newton Stewart, telephone (01671) 2431. This is a seasonal office, so in the winter months you'd need to contact either Dumfries (01387) 53862, or Ayr (01292) 284196.

legend

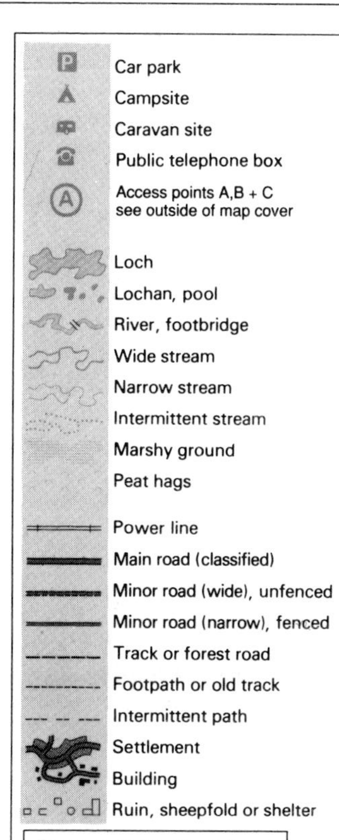

The representation of a road, track or footpath is no evidence of the existence of a right of way

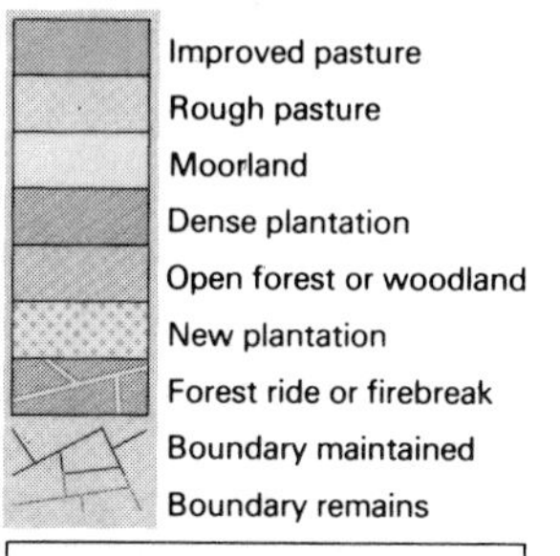

Boundary walls or fences on moorland are shown. Only the walls or fences bounding farmland are shown.

Contour (15m interval)
Index contour (75m interval)
Auxiliary contour
Scattered rock and boulders
Large boulder
Predominantly rocky ground
Major crag
O.S. trig pillar, large cairn
Spot height (from air survey)

Contours change from brown to grey where the ground is predominantly rocky outcrops, small crags and other bare rock.

MAGNETIC NORTH is 5° west of grid north in 1993 decreasing by about 1° in 6 years.

GRID NORTH

Diagrammatic

scale 1:40 000

0 Miles 1

0 Kilometres 1

25 millimetres on the map represents 1000 metres on the ground

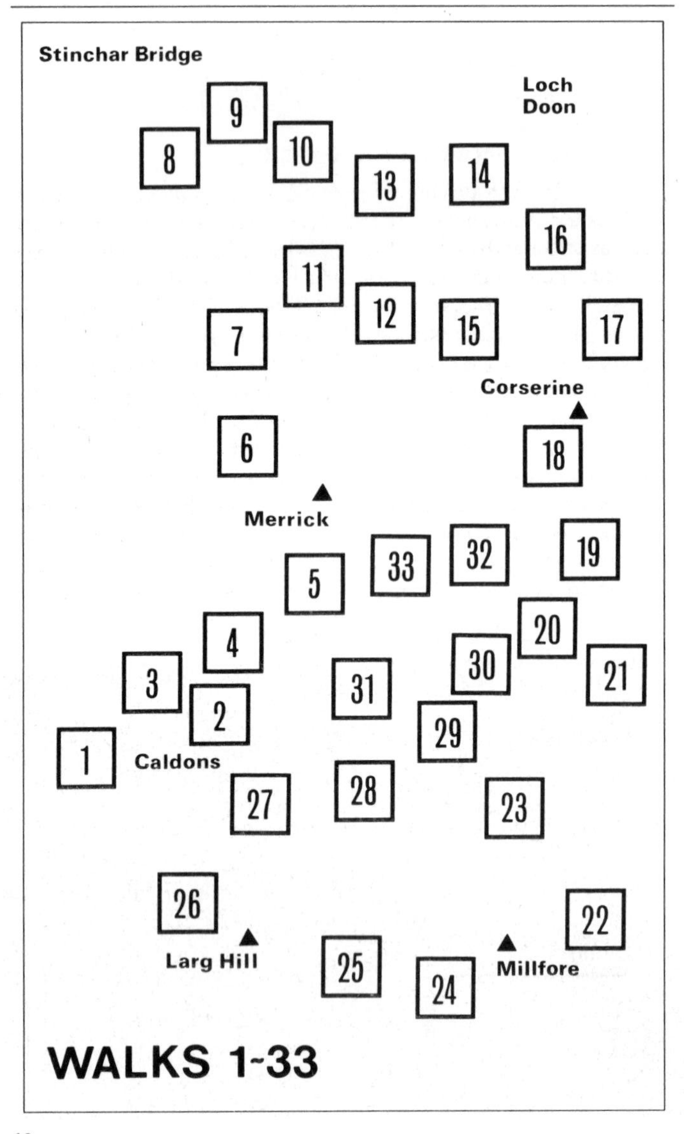
Stinchar Bridge
Loch Doon
9
8
10
13
14
16
11
12
7
15
17
Corserine
6
18
Merrick
33
32
19
5
4
20
3
31
30
21
2
29
1
Caldons
27
28
23
26
22
Larg Hill
25
24
Millfore
WALKS 1-33

Walks

WALK 1: STROAN BRIDGE FOREST TRAILS

There are four colour-coded waymarked trails leaving the Glen Trool Visitor Centre at Stroan Bridge. They are listed on a signboard at the car park nearby and all four trails leave the visitor centre in the same direction. They are, in ascending order of distance: the Red Trail at 1½ miles (2½km); the Blue Trail at 2½ miles (4km); the Yellow Trail at 5 miles (8km); and the White Trail at 6 miles (9½km). It's possible to walk any combination of these trails, but you'll also find that by combining the Yellow Trail and White Trail you'll be covering most of the Red Trail and Blue Trail too. The combined distance is only 7½ miles (12km). Apart from covering each of the short trails, this circuit through the forests of Glen Trool also includes an easy riverside stretch of the long-distance Southern Upland Way. Refreshments and background information can be obtained at the visitor centre, and you could also obtain food and drink at the campsite shop at Caldons half-way round the route.

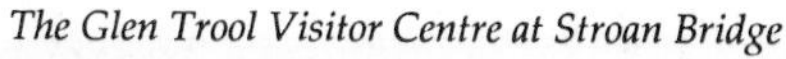

The Glen Trool Visitor Centre at Stroan Bridge

The Route

Distance: An easy 7½ miles (12km) combination of waymarked trails.

Start: At the Glen Trool Visitor Centre - 371786.

Parking: At the visitor centre car park.

Follow the waymarks away from the Glen Trool Visitor Centre. All four trails are routed along the same woodland path at first. The path crosses a forest road, then you turn left along the next forest road. Make sure you're always following yellow markers for the first half of the walk (you'll notice the Red Trail has already gone off a different way). A sign is eventually reached above Stroan House which announces "named species of trees planted within Galloway Forest Park". Have a look round the Tree Plots just off the route, but be sure to come back up to continue along the Yellow Trail. The trail wanders along a forest path above Stroan House and crosses a footbridge below the little waterfall of Spout Head. Eventually, the path descends from the trees to land on the Glen Trool road close to the access road for Caldons Campsite. If you're in need of refreshments then you might be able to get food and drink from the campsite shop, but if you're staying on the route, then follow the access road across the Water of Trool and turn right. You'll still be following yellow markers as well as the "thistle" markers of the Southern Upland Way.

There's an invitation for you to visit the Martyr's Tomb, which is a little way off route in the trees, otherwise simply follow the waymarks out of the tall trees and into a younger plantation with more open views. Parts of the path close to the Water of Trool are boggy and have become overtrodden. Duckboards and little bridges have been installed on some stretches. If you find you need to cut this walk short, then you can cross a footbridge over the Water of Trool and follow a riverside footpath quickly back to the visitor centre. To continue the walk, however, stay on the southern bank of the Water of Trool and start following a series of white markers.

The White Trail stays close to the river, then crosses the river using a bridge on the access road for Holm Farm. The pastoral interlude is brief and the trail turns right and left to enter a stand of tall trees. A path seems to wander almost aimlessly in the forest, following a forest road at one point, then turning right to leave it.

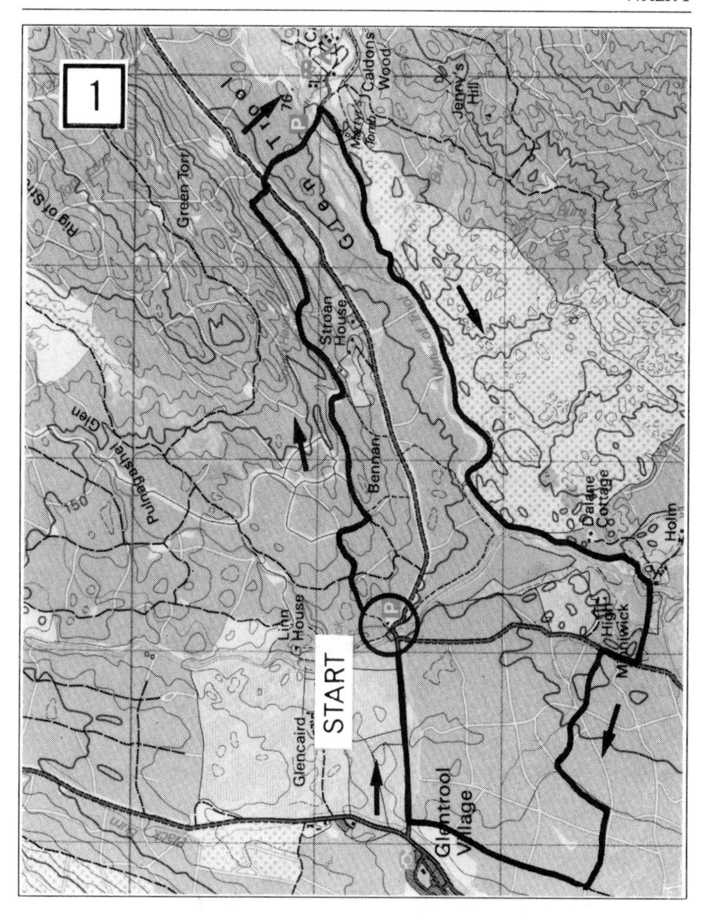

Another forest road is reached in a clear-felled area and the trail turns right to follow it almost to Glentrool Village. A final right turn leads back to the visitor centre. You can avoid walking on the Glen Trool road by following a path through the trees roughly parallel to the road. Use any spare time to explore the deep pools and rocky gorge downstream from Stroan Bridge.

Glen Trool Visitor Centre

A wooden building close to Stroan Bridge serves as a focal point for visitors to Glen Trool. A small information section is stacked with leaflets relevant to the area and large wall panels describe the Galloway Hills, as well as presenting a lively and violent display of Robert the Bruce's ambush of an English force at the Steps of Trool. Teas, snacks and souvenirs are available and the whole enterprise is operated by the Forestry Commission. There are parking and picnicking facilities, while the four colour-coded waymarked forest trails start alongside the centre.

The Tree Plots

The Tree Plots have been planted above Stroan House and were established in the 1950s. Growing trees from around the world are labelled so that visitors can learn to identify the various species which have been planted around the Galloway Forest Park. By visiting the site at different times of the year, visitors can learn to recognise and appreciate the seasonal changes appropriate to each species.

The Martyr's Tomb

A stone stands within a walled enclosure which is signposted from the access road to Caldons Campsite. At that lonely spot six Covenanters were surprised while at prayer and killed by an armed force. The deed was done on 23rd January 1685 during the "Killing Times". Memorials such as this are found throughout Galloway. The stone marking the Martyr's Tomb replaces an earlier slab which is now housed at the museum at Newton Stewart. The original is thought to have been carved by Robert Patterson, who spent most of his life restoring the facing and lettering of those lonely monuments. He received no payment for his self-imposed task, but was never left to go hungry or without lodgings during his labours. A statue of Patterson can be studied at the museum at Newton Stewart, and Walter Scott drew his inspiration for "Old Mortality" from this character.

* * *

WALK 2: LOCH TROOL FOREST TRAIL

The Loch Trool Forest Trail offers a complete circuit of the lovely Loch Trool from either Caldons Campsite or the Bruce's Stone at the end of the Glen Trool road. The entire route is indicated with green waymarks, but the southern half of the route also bears the "thistle"

The Bruce's Stone at the head of Glen Trool

waymarks of the long-distance Southern Upland Way. It's recommended that you start at Caldons Campsite, if only to get the most rugged part of the walk over first. After that, you can study the spot where Robert the Bruce ambushed an English force, as well as having a look at the stone which was placed above the loch to commemorate the event. If the campsite shop is open at Caldons, then you should be able to obtain food and drink either at the beginning or end of the walk.

The Route

Distance: Mostly an easy 5½ mile (9km) waymarked trail.

Start: Near Caldons Campsite - 397791.

Parking: Small parking spaces off the campsite access road.

Park near the bridge over the Water of Trool on the access road to Caldons Campsite. You can either walk to the campsite shop and turn left, or turn left immediately after crossing the Water of Trool and pass the campsite toilet blocks. Either way, you'll pick up the green waymarks of the Loch Trool Forest Trail and the "thistle" markers of the Southern Upland Way - both of which lead away from the campsite and into the surrounding woodlands. There's a great variety of trees to note, with oak dominating the area around the campsite and fine stands of Scots pine deeper into the forest. The trail is easy at first, but soon develops some minor switchback sections. In wet weather there can be muddy patches. A short side-spur from the trail at Torr allows a view across Loch Trool to the distant bulk of Merrick. The trail crosses a steep slope beneath the frowning face of White Bennan, where a signboard explains how Robert the Bruce successfully ambushed an English force in 1307 by rolling boulders onto them.

An easier stretch of the trail leads towards the edge of the forest and gradually down into the glen at Glenhead Burn. The Southern Upland Way turns right, but you cross the footbridge over Glenhead Burn and turn left. Follow the markers, which show a right turn up a field, then a left turn along the access track away from Glenhead. The road runs through a pleasant oakwood and crosses Buchan Bridge, which was "designed and executed by Randolph IX Earl of Galloway AD 1851". There's also a verse carved in stone and a small

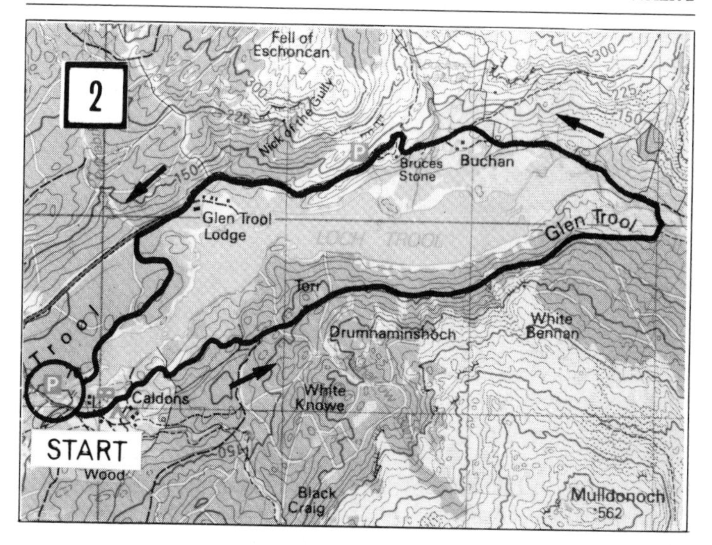

waterfall for you to study. The road runs up past Buchan to reach a car park at the Bruce's Stone. Go up onto the rocky hump where the stone has been sited and enjoy the view over Loch Trool, then turn right to follow a short path to another car park by a toilet block.

Follow the Glen Trool road into the trees and around Glen Trool Lodge. There's no access to the lodge or its grounds, but after passing the entrance gates a waymark on the left reveals a path taking the forest trail off the road. This path wanders into the forests, twists and turns, then crosses a couple of low, forested humps before running closer to the shore of Loch Trool. Shortly afterwards, it follows the Water of Trool and almost immediately lands back on the access road for Caldons Campsite. Before leaving, you might have a look at the Martyr's Tomb which is signposted nearby in the trees on the opposite side of the road.

The Steps of Trool

In 1307, Robert the Bruce secreted his small army on the rugged slopes above Loch Trool and lay in wait for the arrival of a large English force under the command of Aymer de Valance. As the English reached the steep and rocky slopes they were forced to string themselves out and to concentrate on picking their way carefully across. At a signal given by observers on the opposite side of the loch, the Bruce's supporters rolled huge boulders down onto the English, killing some instantly and wounding others. Anyone trying to flee had to do so under a hail of arrows, making the ambush a complete success. The soldiers who were killed in the conflict were buried in the flat ground at the head of Loch Trool, which is known as the Soldier's Holm or Green Acre. The rout of the English force marked a turning point in the fortunes of Robert the Bruce.

The Bruce's Stone

The Bruce's Stone is a fairly recent memorial erected on a rocky prow overlooking Loch Trool, offering a view of the rugged Steps of Trool where the famous ambush took place. It is carved with the words "In loyal remembrance of Robert the Bruce, King of Scots, whose victory in this glen over an English force in March 1307 opened the campaign of independence which he brought to a decisive close at Bannockburn on 24th June 1314". The Bruce's Stone is popular with visitors in Glen Trool and legions of Scottish families have stood proudly beside it for pictures which later grace the walls and mantelshelves of many homes.

* * *

WALK 3: FELL OF ESCHONCAN AND PULNAGASHEL

The Fell of Eschoncan is really only a minor height when compared with the rest of the Galloway Hills, but it positively looms over the car park at the Bruce's Stone. It seems almost unassailable to mere walkers, but in fact it can be climbed by a short, steep path. You could use this approach as an alternative way of climbing Merrick, or simply enjoy the ascent for its own sake. There are splendid views over Glen Trool from the top of the hill. It's possible to link into a network of forest roads leading down towards Stroan Bridge and the Glen Trool Visitor Centre. You could break for refreshments at the visitor centre around the half-way mark, then follow a series of colour-coded waymarked forest trails back to the Bruce's Stone at the head of Glen Trool.

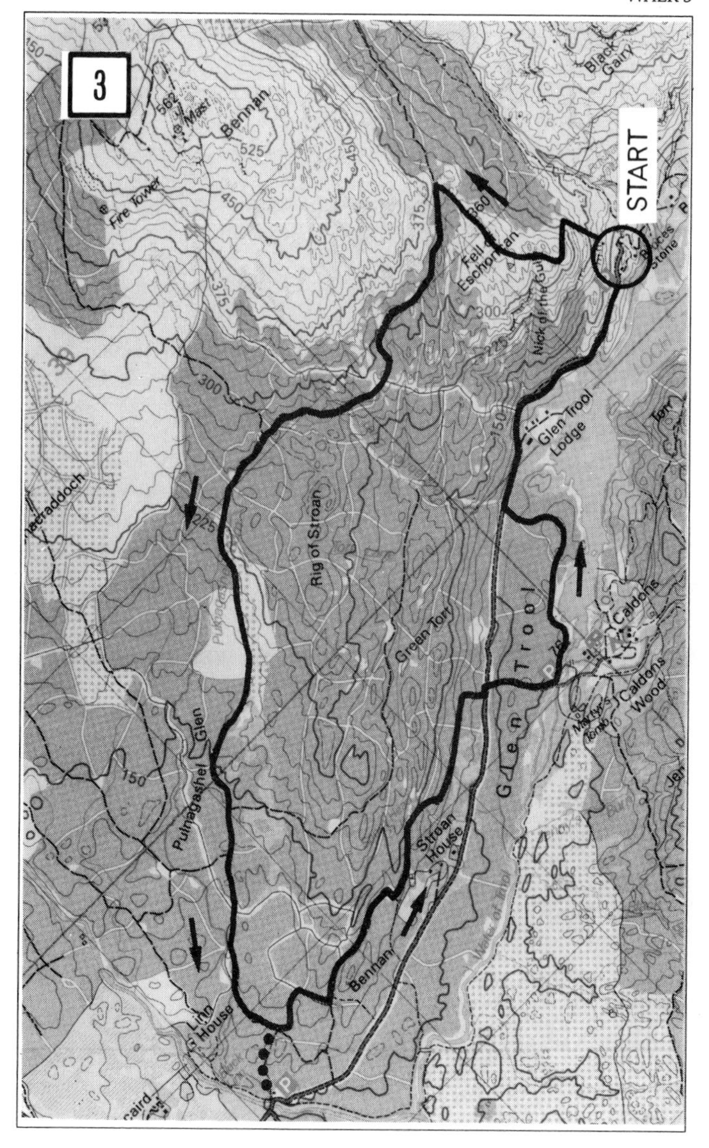
3
START
Black Gairy
Bennan
Mast
Fire Tower
Fell of Eschoncan
Bruces Stone
Glen Trool Lodge
Rig of Stroan
Green Tory
Glen Trool
Caldons
Caldons Wood
Martyr's Tomb
Stroan House
Bennan
Pulnagashel Glen
Linn House

The Route

Distance: An easy $8^{1/2}$ mile (14km) walk with a steep and rugged start.

Start: At the Bruce's Stone - 415804.

Parking: At the car park by the Bruce's Stone.

Park at the end of the Glen Trool road, close to the Bruce's Stone. If the last space is full, then park just before at another car park by a toilet block. There's a sign at the end of the road which announces the start of the Merrick climb, but you don't go along that broad path. Instead, look to the left of the sign for a narrow and inconspicuous little path leaving the car park unannounced. This little path leads up the Fell of Eschoncan, rising steeply through bracken at first to reach the corner of a young forestry plantation at a higher level. At the forest edge, the path swings round to the left and the brackeny slopes are replaced by slopes of tussocky grass and heather. Follow the narrow path ever upwards, passing a couple of large rocks and keeping a step or two back from a steep, rugged brow. The view along Glen Trool opens up dramatically as height is gained and there's a panoramic view from a cairn. The grass and heather cover is shorter on the hummocky top of the fell, though there are squelchy patches of ground too. You can make a short detour from the path to include the 347m trig point. A tall cairn is passed just before the path runs off the fell onto a forest road.

Turn left to follow the forest road. Views are immediately restricted, but progress downhill is rapid and gently graded. Be sure to turn left at the next junction of forest roads, then avoid the next turning left and the next turning right down in the lower parts of Pulnagashel Glen. You'll be walking fairly close to Pulnagashel Burn on the lower part of the forest road, then the road drifts away from the water. You quickly reach a point where four colour-coded waymarked forest trails cross the forest road. A right turn at this point gives access to the Glen Trool Visitor Centre where you could break for teas and snacks, but to continue the walk you should turn left to follow the waymarked trails towards the head of Glen Trool.

Follow yellow waymarks at first - at least as far as Caldons Campsite. A path leads through the forest, then you turn left along the next forest road. A sign is eventually reached which announces "named species of trees planted within Galloway Forest Park".

Have a look round the Tree Plots just off the route, but be sure to come back up to continue along the Yellow Trail. The trail wanders along a forest path above Stroan House and crosses a footbridge below the little waterfall of Spout Head. Eventually, the path descends from the trees to land on the Glen Trool road close to the access road for Caldons Campsite. If you're in need of refreshments then you might be able to get food and drink from the campsite shop, but if you're staying on the route, then turn left before crossing the bridge over the Water of Trool.

Green waymarks show the course of the Loch Trool Forest Trail, which leads back to the Bruce's Stone. Follow the Water of Trool upstream and walk along the forested shore of Loch Trool. The trail leads away from the shore, crosses a couple of low, forested humps, then twists and turns and eventually lands on the Glen Trool road. Turn right to follow the road around Glen Trool Lodge. There's no access to the lodge or its grounds. The road emerges from the trees beneath the Fell of Eschoncan, close to the Bruce's Stone and car parks.

The Fell of Eschoncan

The Fell of Eschoncan dominates the head of Glen Trool and some visitors have been known to believe it was actually Merrick. Once you've walked over the hill and enjoyed the panorama around the glen, you might wonder whether it ever supported any type of promontory fort or similar settlement. Well, a small horde of Bronze Age implements were found on the hill in the 1940s, but nothing else has ever been discovered to suggest any sort of settlement.

* * *

WALK 4: BENNAN AND THE FELL OF ESCHONCAN

Bennan is a fairly modest height which is mostly forested, but it has rugged, grassy and rocky slopes finally rising to its summit. A radio mast has been planted on the top of the hill, so it is immediately recognisable in distant views and is something of a landmark. An extension of the forest road network above Glen Trool serves the radio mast, but there is no general access for vehicles. All the same, bear the road in mind if you're ever caught late at night on Merrick and would like to take a safe course back down into the glen. The

Merrick path is used at the start of this walk, then you head off for the summit of Bennan instead. After climbing Bennan, the Fell of Eschoncan can be used as a stepping-stone on the way back down to the head of Glen Trool.

The Route

Distance: A moderate hill walk of 7½ miles (12km).

Start: At the Bruce's Stone - 415804.

Parking: At the car park by the Bruce's Stone.

Park at the end of the Glen Trool road, close to the Bruce's Stone. If the last space is full, then park just before at another car park by a toilet block. There's a sign at the end of the road which announces the start of the Merrick climb, with a broad path leading up a rugged slope. Follow this path, which crosses bouldery ground close to

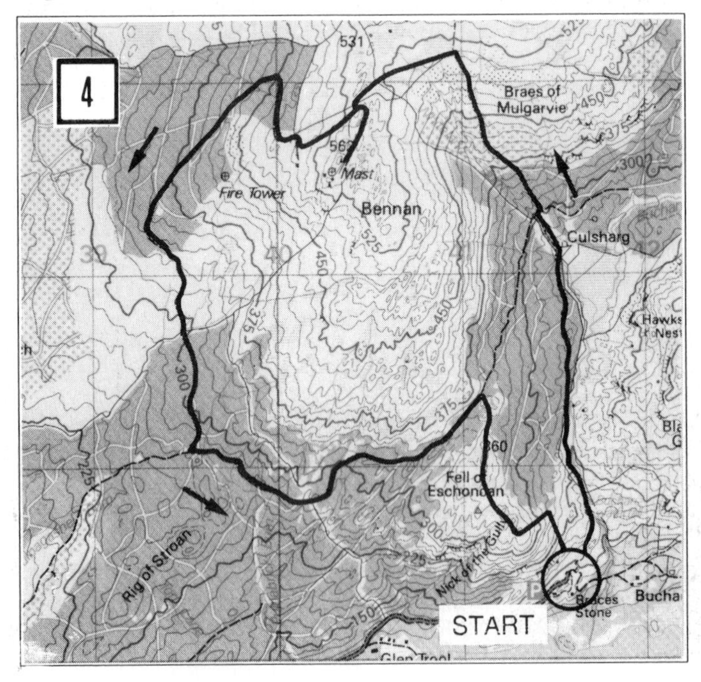

Buchan Burn. Enjoy small waterfalls and occasional trees before the path climbs grass and heather slopes to a forest. A forest path leading onwards used to be a mess, but it has recently been resurfaced and is much better underfoot. The path emerges briefly into a clearing by the Culsharg Bothy. The path runs uphill into the forest again, running close to Whiteland Burn. A forest road bridge is used to cross the burn, then the path is signposted further uphill alongside the burn. After running up through a younger plantation the path reaches a forest fence, where you cross a stile to reach the open hillside.

Bear left and continue uphill at a gentle gradient away from the path, to reach a wall on the hillside. Go through a gap in the wall, then follow a fence on the left, crossing it when you're close to the gravel road on Bennan. Simply follow this road a short way uphill to reach the radio mast on the 562m summit. Turn around and follow the gravel road back downhill to start the descent. The road describes a sort of broad spiral around the upper half of Bennan and quickly runs down into forests. The forest road keeps descending until it reaches a small burn in a clear-felled area. There's a slight rise

Culsharg Bothy beside the path to Merrick

beyond, then the road goes downhill again. Make a left turn at a junction of forest roads and follow the other road uphill. Keep going along this road until the forest thins out on a high gap. A cairn on the right side of the road shows a gap in the trees where a path leads onto the Fell of Eschoncan.

The narrow path passes a tall cairn on the hummocky crest of the Fell of Eschoncan, then you could detour towards the 347m trig point if you wanted. The shorter grass and heather cover on the top of the fell has some squelchy patches, then as a cairn is reached there are panoramic views over Glen Trool. Head off to the left, following the path down near a steep, rugged brow, passing a couple of large rocks on the way to the top corner of a young forestry plantation. The grass is more tussocky and the heather deeper on the descent, but once the forest is reached there is tall bracken cover instead. Swing to the right at the forest edge and continue steeply downhill to arrive in the car park close to the Bruce's Stone.

The Culsharg Bothy

The Culsharg Bothy was formerly an isolated shepherd's house with near neighbours in Glen Trool. It now stands in a small clearing almost surrounded by forestry. Its empty window-holes face Buchan Hill and there is a memorial cairn off to one side. Although the roof has been replaced, there are no doors or windows in the bothy, so it really offers no more than an emergency shelter. You couldn't rely on it to keep out the wind, rain or midges. Despite its shortcoming, it has a fireplace and generally shows signs of recent use, though you'd have to bring your own wood for the fire. Technically, its rooms could hold quite a few walkers, but if driving rain came in through the empty window- and door-holes, then sheltered space could be very limited. It's a place to remember in case of desperation if ever you're coming down from the hills on a filthy night and have no hope of reaching any better shelter.

❊ ❊ ❊

WALK 5: MERRICK AND LOCH ENOCH

Merrick is the highest of the Galloway Hills - in fact it's the highest hill in southern Scotland. It's also the hub of the Range of the Awful Hand, so there are many ways of extending a walk from the summit into the wild country beyond. There's a popular line of ascent from

The head of Loch Trool from the forest trail
Benyellary and Merrick from the Fell of Eschoncan

Merrick and the silver sands of Loch Enoch
Black Gairy and Merrick from Kirshinnoch Burn

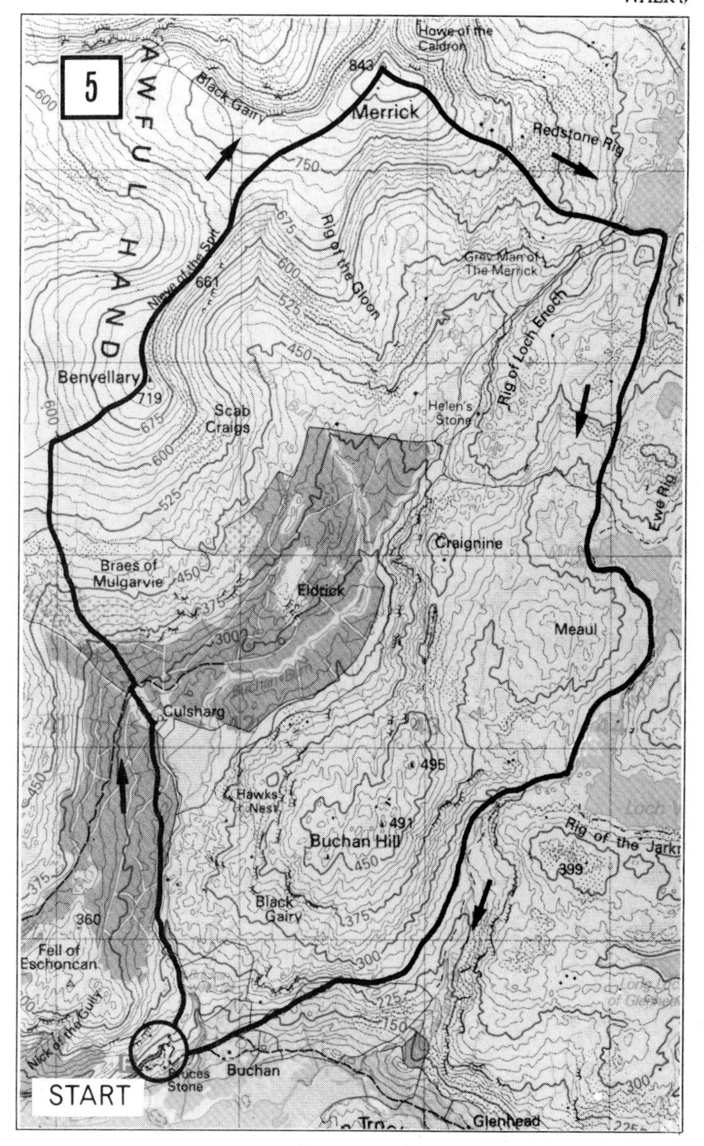
5
AWFUL HAND
Howe of the Caldron
843
Merrick
Black Gairy
Redstone Rig
750
675
Rig of the Gloon
Grey Man of The Merrick
Nieve of the Spit
661
600
525
Rig of Loch Enoch
450
Benyellary
719
Scab Craigs
Helen's Stone
Ewe Rig
Craignine
Braes of Mulgarvie
Eldrick
Meaul
Culsharg
495
Hawks Nest
491
Buchan Hill
Rig of the Jarkr
399
Black Gairy
360
Fell of Eschoncan
Nick of the Gully
Bruces Stone
Buchan
START
Glenhead

the Bruce's Stone at the head of Glen Trool, and many walkers use this on a first-time visit. Having gained the summit of Merrick, some walkers will turn around and come back down the same way, while a few hardy souls will head deeper into the wild country beyond. Most walkers who attempt a circular walk will descend towards Loch Enoch, Loch Neldricken and Loch Valley before following Gairland Burn down into Glen Trool. This is the circuit offered below. In clear weather, you'd be inclined to linger on the summit and enjoy the remarkably extensive view which stretches from the Highlands of Scotland to Northern England and Northern Ireland.

The Route

Distance: A difficult 9 mile (15km) walk mostly on paths.

Start: At the Bruce's Stone - 415804.

Parking: At the car park by the Bruce's Stone.

Park at the end of the Glen Trool road, close to the Bruce's Stone. If the last space is full, then park just before at another car park by a toilet block. There's a sign at the end of the road which announces the start of the Merrick climb, with a broad path leading up a rugged slope. Follow this path, which crosses bouldery ground close to Buchan Burn. Enjoy small waterfalls and occasional trees before the path climbs grass and heather slopes to a forest. A forest path leading onwards used to be a mess, but it has recently been resurfaced and is much better underfoot. The path emerges briefly into a clearing by the Culsharg Bothy. The path runs uphill into the forest again, running close to Whiteland Burn. A forest road bridge is used to cross the burn, then the path is signposted further uphill alongside the burn. After running up through a younger plantation the path reaches a forest fence, where you cross a stile to reach the open hillside.

Head straight up the hillside, following the path towards a wall. The path swings to the right as it runs alongside the wall and continues to the 719m summit of Benyellary. This has small outcrops of rock and a summit cairn - proving to be a handy place for a break while studying the immense bulk of Merrick ahead. Keep following the wall along a grassy ridge called the Nieve of the Spit. Part of the ridge is muddy where water seeps across the path. Just beyond that point, the path swings off to the right, away from the wall, to climb an open grassy slope. This is pitched at a fairly gentle gradient and the path passes odd large boulders. The path crosses short grass and eventually levels out on the broad hilltop where there's a large cairn and a trig point at 843m. The cairn has been fashioned into a wind shelter. Although the Galloway Hills are generally quiet, a fine summer day will find a small crowd of walkers on the summit of Merrick.

After sampling the views - if you've been blessed with clear weather - you can head roughly eastwards to overlook Loch Enoch. The remarkable shoreline features headlands and bays, with islets and rocks marooned above the surface of the water. Aim for the southern end of the loch by walking down a reasonably easy grassy slope at first. As progress is made downhill, you'll find the ground becomes more and more rugged and you'll have to detour around short, steep sections and minor outcrops of rock. There's a final steep step down to a wall and fence close to the shore of Loch Enoch, then you need to follow the shore a short way beyond the wall and fence.

Head southwards away from the shore of Loch Enoch, walking uphill a short way to pass through a rugged little gap near Craig Neldricken. There is a path, but it isn't very clear in places, which keeps down in a small valley scattered throughout with boulders. As the path descends, it crosses squelchy areas of boggy ground. If you keep an eye peeled you'll notice Loch Arron off to the left, but you don't go out to it. The path drops down to cross a ruined wall on the way to Loch Neldricken. The first little bay of the loch is known as the Murder Hole. There's a choice of routes ahead. One boggy path goes over the rise of Meaul, but it's more interesting to stay close to the shore of Loch Neldricken, noting how shallow the water is in many places. Numerous rocks peep above the water, while the southern end is clogged with weeds. Mid Burn tumbles down across bare rock and boulders, passing an old stone sheepfold on its way to Loch Valley. Rugged grass and heather proves to be boggy underfoot, but forge onwards to follow the path alongside Loch Valley.

The water leaving Loch Valley is Gairland Burn and this is followed closely in its upper reaches. The accompanying path is quite boggy and muddy in places, but boulders make useful stepping-stones. Later, a firm path descends gently through a grassy valley, moving away from Gairland Burn and later crossing slopes of bracken. The path runs alongside a wall, then goes through a small swing-gate to enter large hillside fields. After heading diagonally across the field, a wall is followed down to a stile so that you land on the rough road near Buchan. Keep right to follow the road into a little oakwood and across Buchan Bridge. There's a little waterfall to study and a few words carved in stone on either side of the bridge. The road continues through the wood and emerges to make a final zig-zag up to the car park by the Bruce's Stone.

The View from Merrick

As the accompanying diagram displays, the panoramic view from Merrick stretches across the Highlands and Islands of Scotland, to the Antrim and Mourne Mountains of Northern Ireland, to the Isle of Man and the distant fells of the English Lake District.

Furthermore, on a clear night you can test your navigational ability to the limit and see how many lighthouses you can identify, as well as noting constellations of towns and villages. It's surprising how many visitors point to the Mull of Kintyre and call it the Mull of Galloway, or mistake the Isle of Man for Ireland. Although similar views can be obtained from other heights, the view from Merrick seems to be the most extensive. The major heights noted on the diagram are the limits observed by the author, though in crystal clear conditions it might be possible to see much more distant features. Regarding comments on night-time viewing, the author has camped on the summit of Merrick - and has even been provided with a cooked breakfast by two other gentlemen who also took a notion to pitch their tent on the hill for the night!

The Grey Man

The Grey Man of Merrick is a natural feature you can discover quite easily. Follow a ruined wall and fence away from Loch Enoch, noting how the two lines diverge slightly as they cross a rise. They come close together as they descend, and at that point you should study a rockface off to the right. From the right angle, there really is a face seen in profile and this is the Grey Man of Merrick. He has, incidentally, also given his name to a walking club from Ayr which regularly organises walks in the Galloway Hills.

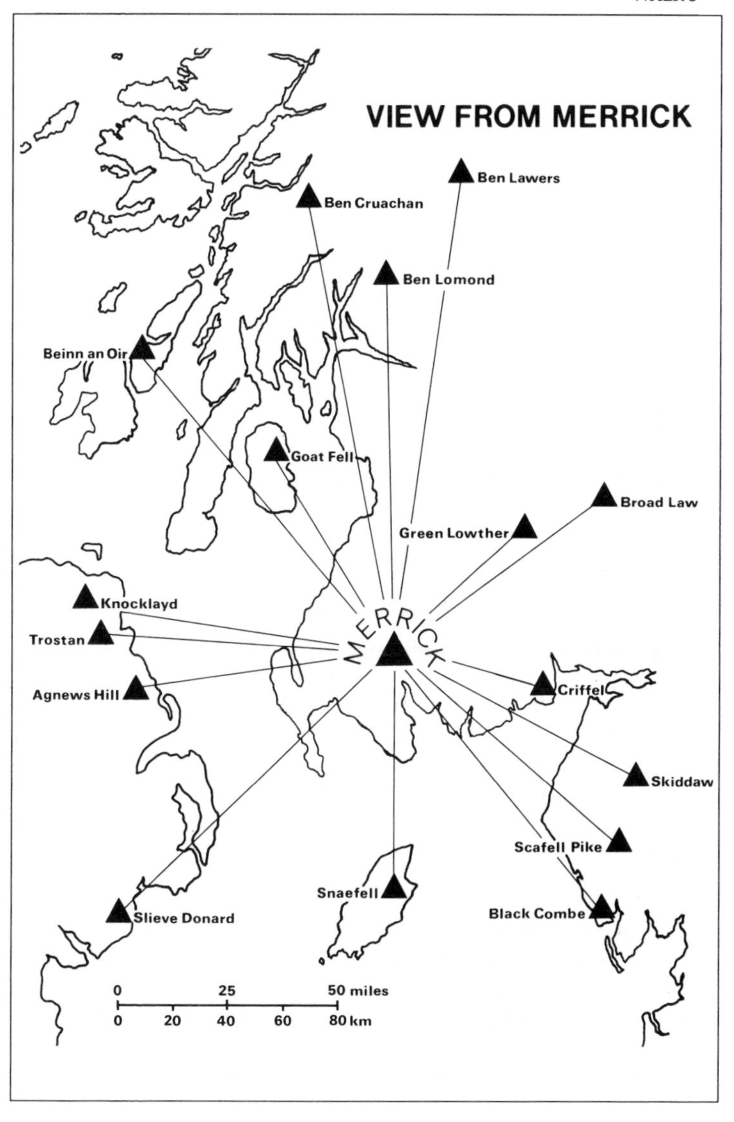
VIEW FROM MERRICK
Ben Lawers
Ben Cruachan
Ben Lomond
Beinn an Oir
Goat Fell
Broad Law
Green Lowther
Knocklayd
Trostan
MERRICK
Agnews Hill
Criffel
Skiddaw
Scafell Pike
Snaefell
Black Combe
Slieve Donard
0
25
50 miles
0
20
40
60
80 km

A vegetated corner of Loch Neldricken

The Murder Hole

In S.R.Crockett's novel The Raiders *the notorious Murder Hole is off to one side of Loch Neldricken. You'll find it is named on maps and you can look into its depths and wonder how many unfortunate wretches were killed and dumped there. In fact, no-one was. Crockett seems to have placed the Murder Hole by Loch Neldricken simply because of its wild and desolate location. The original Murder Hole was far away over the Range of the Awful Hand near Rowantree Toll on the Glentrool Village to Straiton road. All the same, in a remote place such as this you can let your imagination run riot - as Crockett must have done. He is known to have stayed at Glenhead, at the head of Glen Trool, during the course of his writings and no doubt he made excursions into these wild hills to seek inspirational themes and stories. Another property attached to the Murder Hole is that it never freezes over, which is something you can check during the next cold snap.*

* * *

WALK 6: MERRICK AND KIRRIEREOCH HILL

There are a couple of good ridge routes which can be used to approach Merrick from the western side, though you first have to negotiate forestry plantations around Kirriereoch. Until fairly recently, walkers could use the Wigwam Bothy as a base for climbing Merrick, Kirriereoch Hill and Tarfessock, but the bothy was destroyed by fire and may not be replaced. The forest road which was used to reach the bothy can, of course, still be used and it offers a quick way in and out of the forestry plantation. After the long walk-in, you can get straight onto the open hillside and tackle a splendid horseshoe walk which has Merrick at its head. The neighbouring Kirriereoch Hill can be climbed afterwards and there's no reason why you shouldn't extend the walk by including Tarfessock too.

The Route

Distance: A fairly difficult hill walk of 12½ miles (20km).
Start: Kirriereoch Picnic Site - 359866.
Parking: At the Kirriereoch Picnic Site.

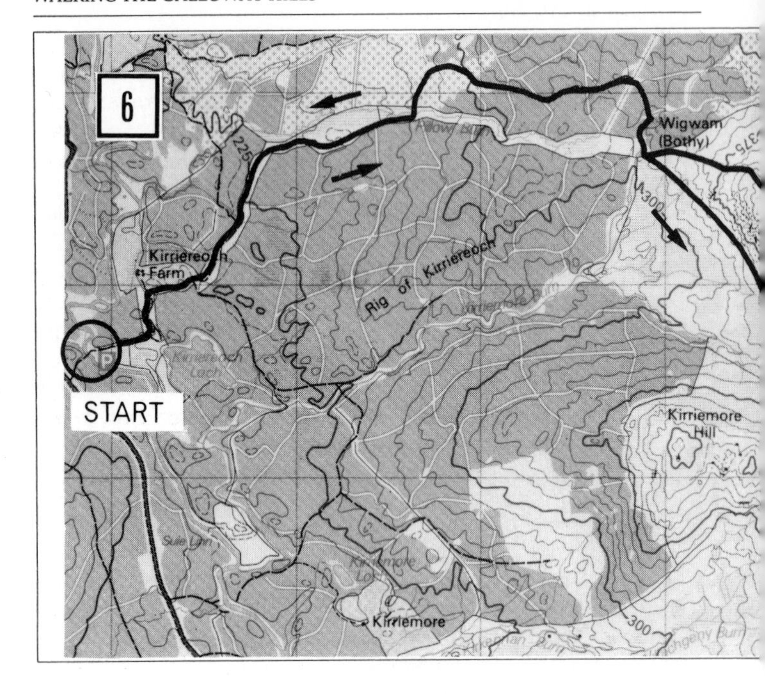

A Forestry Commission sign stands by the Glentrool Village to Straiton road and indicates the picnic site at Kirriereoch. Simply drive a short way down the forest road and park by a bridge over the Water of Minnoch. There's an unplanted area of bog by the river, but for the early part of the walk you'll be wandering through forestry plantations. Follow the forest road on foot away from the picnic site. Before long, a sign on the right indicates Kirriereoch Loch, which you could view by making a short detour across a stile. You may be able to see Merrick in the distance before returning to the forest road. Turn right at a gateway before reaching Kirriereoch Farm. There's a sign at this junction for Tarfessock, but be sure to keep left at the next junction of forest roads. There's a wide, unplanted, rushy swathe which takes the forest road onwards towards the hills. When the Tarfessock road later goes off to the left to a farm of that name, be sure to continue straight onwards instead.

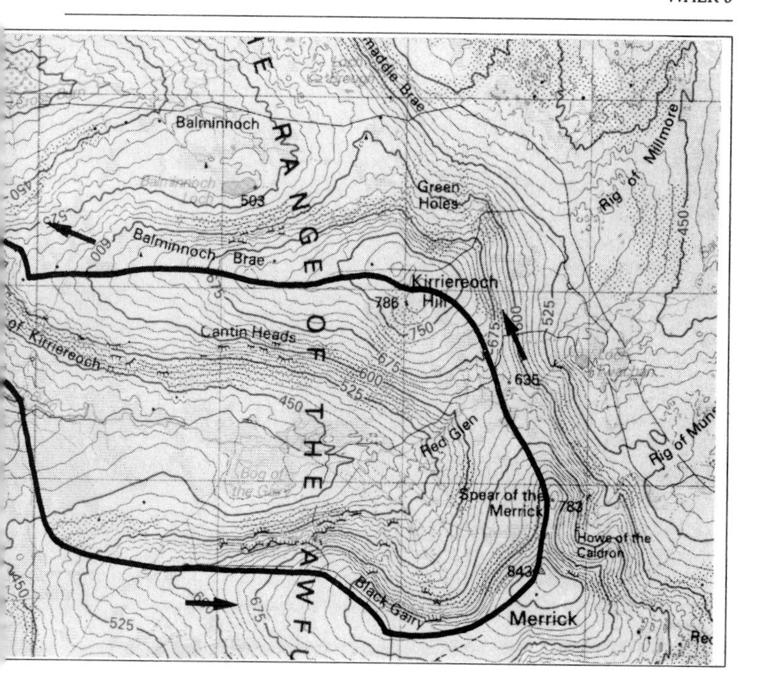

The forest road reaches a clear-felled area and crosses over Pillow Burn. Simply follow the forest road uphill at a gentle angle to its very end.

Drop down to the right at the end of the forest road and you'll find a path leading into the forest. This was the approach route for the Wigwam Bothy and there are some muddy patches to negotiate. Also watch for slippery tree roots. When you emerge from the forest, find a way over Cross Burn, then walk downstream past the ruined base of the Wigwam Bothy. Bear to the left around the edge of the forest and use a small stile to cross the forest fence at one corner.

There's hardly any path trodden across the broad, boggy valley of Kirshinnoch Burn. You'll find that the easiest course is to stay a little up on the slope below the Torrs of Kirriereoch. There is plenty of tussocky grass and heather to slow your progress, but ultimately you'll reach the banks of Kirshinnoch Burn. There is a vague path trodden alongside the burn. Aim to cross the burn to reach a point where there's a hole in the corner of a wall. This gives way to a fairly flat, rushy, boggy area. Forge straight across this and climb up the rugged slope beyond. Swing to the left and try to keep to the broad crest of the ridge. There is grass and heather which is scattered throughout with boulders. There are fewer rocks once a minor hump has been crossed - the one with a ruined wall crossing just beyond. The grass is shorter, so the walking is easier, but there's a lengthy slope to be climbed to reach the top of Black Gairy. In mist, a ruined wall on the northern side of the ridge proves to be a faultless guide. Cross over the ruined wall on the top of Black Gairy before it swings off to the right. Head across a broad gap where a steep drop falls away to the Bog of the Gairy. An intermittent path leads around the top of the steep slope and rises easily to the 843m summit of Merrick. There's a trig point and a large cairn which has been fashioned into a wind shelter.

After enjoying the wide-ranging views in clear weather, or morosely contemplating a map in thick mist, leave the summit of Merrick in a northerly direction. Walk down a steep, blunt ridge onto the little hump called the Spear of Merrick at 783m. Pass the small cairn at this point and continue down a longer, steeper and rockier slope to reach a broad gap bearing a patch of bog at 635m. Cross the gap and climb past outcrops of rock and a ruined wall. As progress is made uphill, the grass gets shorter and there are simply a few odd boulders scattered around. The summit of Kirriereoch Hill is 786m, but there are two cairns - one small one on the very top of the hill and a larger one off to one side which has been made into a small shelter. The broad summit area is gently undulating and is crossed by a ruined wall.

The wall provides the key to the descent. Simply follow it westwards along the broad crest of Balminnoch Brae. The smooth, grassy ridge leads gently downhill at first, passing an occasional boulder. After crossing a vague rise, the wall continues downhill and the grass becomes rougher and interspersed with rocks. There's a sudden corner in the wall, at which point you leave it and follow a line of old fenceposts along the ridge instead. Note a right turn at a prominent boulder - the Carnirock Stone - then later swing to the

Kirriereoch Loch and a distant view of Merrick

left to keep the line of posts in sight as you pick a way down a rugged ridge of grass and heather. The posts can be traced down to a boggy area and you should aim for a corner of the forest fence and cross a small stile there.

You're now on the line which was used earlier in the day's walk, so all you need to do is to retrace your steps to the start of the walk at the Kirriereoch Picnic Site. Follow Cross Burn upstream past the ruined base of the Wigwam Bothy and find a way across. Locate the muddy path which runs into the trees to emerge on the forest road above. Turn left to follow the forest road back to the Kirriereoch Picnic Site to complete the walk-out.

The Wigwam Bothy

The Wigwam Bothy was unique, but is sadly no longer in existence and may not be replaced in the future. It had the shape of a wigwam, but was made of wood with a central stove inside. It was raised on a supporting ring of concrete blocks and was originally placed below the Range of the Awful Hand for the use of foresters. It became quite popular with walkers and certainly saved having to repeat the long walk-in from the Kirriereoch

Picnic Site. Some people believe it was deliberately burnt to the ground, and some walkers who were unaware of its fate have been seriously inconvenienced by its loss. A note in the bothy book at White Laggan recorded one group's experiences. They had walked to Tunskeen one afternoon and arrived to find the roof had been blown off. Somewhat disappointed, they crossed the Range of the Awful Hand to reach the Wigwam in the evening - to find it burnt to the ground. They crossed Merrick in darkness in poor weather and arrived at White Laggan in the wee small hours. They closed the account of their experiences with a line or two which must be heavily edited, wishing that the arsonists could be made to walk as far as they had walked that night, with red-hot pokers up their backsides!

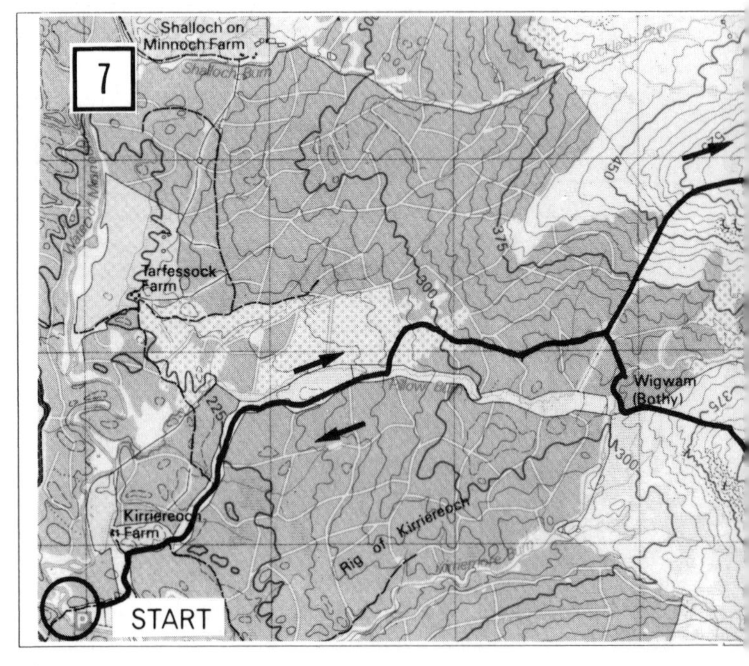

WALK 7: TARFESSOCK AND KIRRIEREOCH HILL

There are some good ridge routes leading onto the Range of the Awful Hand from the western side, though you first have to find a way through the forestry plantations around the Kirriereoch Picnic Site. Both Tarfessock and Kirriereoch Hill can be climbed using the rugged western ridges, which can be used to create a horseshoe walk. It's also possible to head off along the main ridge to Shalloch on Minnoch or Merrick. Since the Wigwam Bothy was destroyed by fire, there is no longer a handy base for walkers on this side of the hills, but the forest road which ran close to the bothy can still be used for the walk-in. Once clear of the trees, the hillsides lead up to the summits and you have the freedom to wander in any direction.

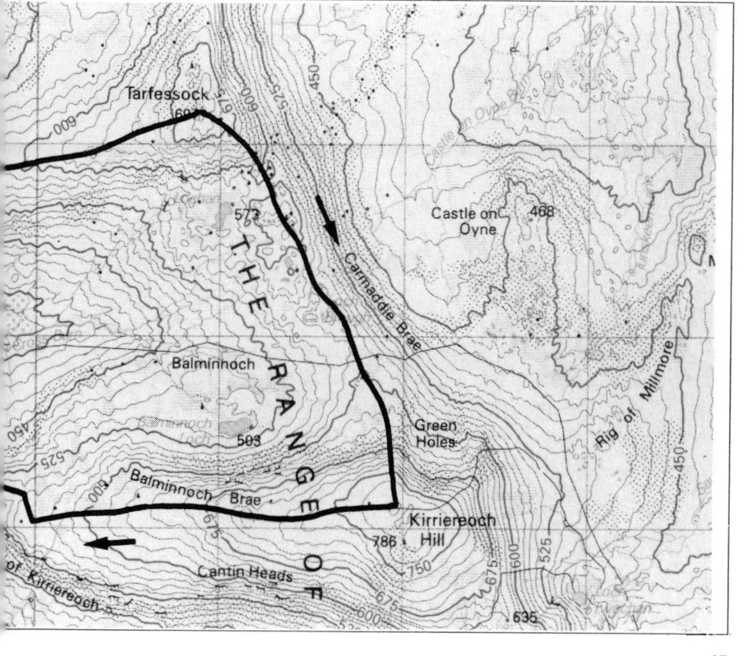

The Route

Distance: A fairly difficult hill walk of 12 miles (19km).

Start: Kirriereoch Picnic Site - 359866.

Parking: At the Kirriereoch Picnic Site.

A Forestry Commission sign stands by the Glentrool Village to Straiton road and indicates the picnic site at Kirriereoch. Simply drive a short way down the forest road and park by a bridge over the Water of Minnoch. There's an unplanted area of bog by the river, but for the early part of the walk you'll be wandering through forestry plantations. Follow the forest road on foot away from the picnic site. Before long, a sign on the right indicates Kirriereoch Loch, which you could view by making a short detour across a stile. You may be able to see Merrick in the distance before returning to the forest road. Turn right at a gateway before reaching Kirriereoch Farm. There's a sign at this junction for Tarfessock, but be sure to keep left at the next junction of forest roads. There's a wide, unplanted, rushy swathe which takes the forest road onwards towards the hills. When the Tarfessock road later goes off to the left to a farm of that name, be sure to continue straight onwards instead. The forest road reaches a clear-felled area and crosses over Pillow Burn. Simply follow the forest road uphill at a gentle angle to its very end.

Turn left at the end of the forest road and walk uphill. There's the remains of an old post and wire fence leading up a fairly wide forest ride. Be careful not to trip over loops of old wire hidden in the rugged vegetation. As you emerge at the top edge of the forest, the fence swings off to the left, but you should continue straight onwards and upwards. There are all sorts of vaguely trodden paths on this ascent, but you should use only those which follow the broad crest of Tarfessock. There are odd cairns along the crest, but they don't seem intended to mark a course for walkers to follow. Eventually, you'll reach the summit cairn which stands at 697m on top of a low, rocky outcrop.

Leave the summit of Tarfessock by walking roughly south-eastwards along the main crest of the Range of the Awful Hand. The rugged descent is neither too steep nor too long, but it leads down to a broad, hummocky, lochan-strewn gap which could be a problem to walk across in poor visibility. In fine weather, however, you can enjoy the views over the Carmaddie Brae into the wild heartlands of the Galloway Hills. After passing little Loch Brough, cross a fence and start to climb up the steep, stony northern face of Kirriereoch Hill. The ascent is hard work, but it is soon over and the ground levels out in a broad area of short grass. A ruined wall crosses the top of the hill, and you'll cross this if you want to reach the 786m summit of Kirriereoch Hill. There are two cairns - one small one on the very top of the hill and a larger one off to one side which has been made into a small shelter. Return to the ruined wall.

The wall provides the key to the descent. Simply follow it westwards along the broad crest of Balminnoch Brae. The smooth, grassy ridge leads gently downhill at first, passing an occasional boulder. After crossing a vague rise, the wall continues downhill and the grass becomes rougher and interspersed with rocks. There's a sudden corner in the wall, at which point you leave it and follow a line of old fenceposts along the ridge instead. Note a right turn at a prominent boulder, the Carnirock Stone, then later swing to the left to keep the line of posts in sight as you pick a way down a rugged ridge of grass and heather. The posts can be traced down to a boggy area and you should aim for a corner of the forest fence and cross a small stile there.

Follow Cross Burn upstream to pass the ruined base of the Wigwam Bothy and find a way across. Locate the muddy path which runs into the trees to emerge on the forest road above. You're now on the line which was used earlier in the day's walk, so all you need to do is to turn left and retrace your earlier steps along the forest road to return to the Kirriereoch Picnic Site to complete the walk-out.

The Range of the Awful Hand

While walking on the western flanks of the Range of the Awful Hand you might take a step back from the hills and wonder at the rather fanciful name of the range. You have to step well back at least to a good viewpoint on the Glentrool Village to Straiton road, so that you can see the entire range in one sweeping glance. You have to imagine that the ridges leading from the main ridge are actually fingers attached to an enormous hand which is firmly clamped down on the Galloway countryside. Starting from the north, Shalloch on Minnoch is the little finger, followed by the ring finger of Tarfessock, then Kirriereoch Hill, with Merrick forming a huge forefinger. The thumb of the Awful Hand is the side-summit of Benyellary. Maybe you'll be convinced that you can see the Awful Hand, or maybe you won't be at all impressed, but that is the commonly related explanation for the name of the range.

* * *

WALK 8: CORNISH HILL AND SHALLOCH ON MINNOCH

The Forestry Commission has established a couple of easy waymarked walks which start from the car park above Stinchar Bridge. One of the trails wanders downstream alongside the River Stinchar in search of Stinchar Falls. The other one wanders upstream, then climbs over the rugged little height of Cornish Hill. The Cornish Hill Walk can be used as a stepping-stone to reach the lonely whaleback rise of Shalloch on Minnoch. The approach to the big hill is both boggy and rocky in places, with deep and difficult vegetation to negotiate. However, there is a fairly straightforward return route over North Top and Cairnadloch. Although the outward and return legs are quite close together, they traverse remarkably different terrains.

The Route

Distance: A difficult hill walk of 7½ miles (12km).

Start: At Stinchar Bridge - 397957.

Parking: At the car park just above Stinchar Bridge.

Starting from the car park just above Stinchar Bridge, walkers are sent off in two directions. The Cornish Hill Walk is signposted as being over the footbridge on the River Stinchar. Marker posts topped with white paint indicate the line of the walk, but in any case it's initially routed along a clear pathway through the forest. This has been recently realigned to cut out some overtrodden parts, with some stretches being surfaced in wood chippings. After wandering gently uphill for a while, the path crosses the River Stinchar using another footbridge and continues past the ruins of Craiglure Lodge. After another gentle climb uphill the path reaches the edge of the

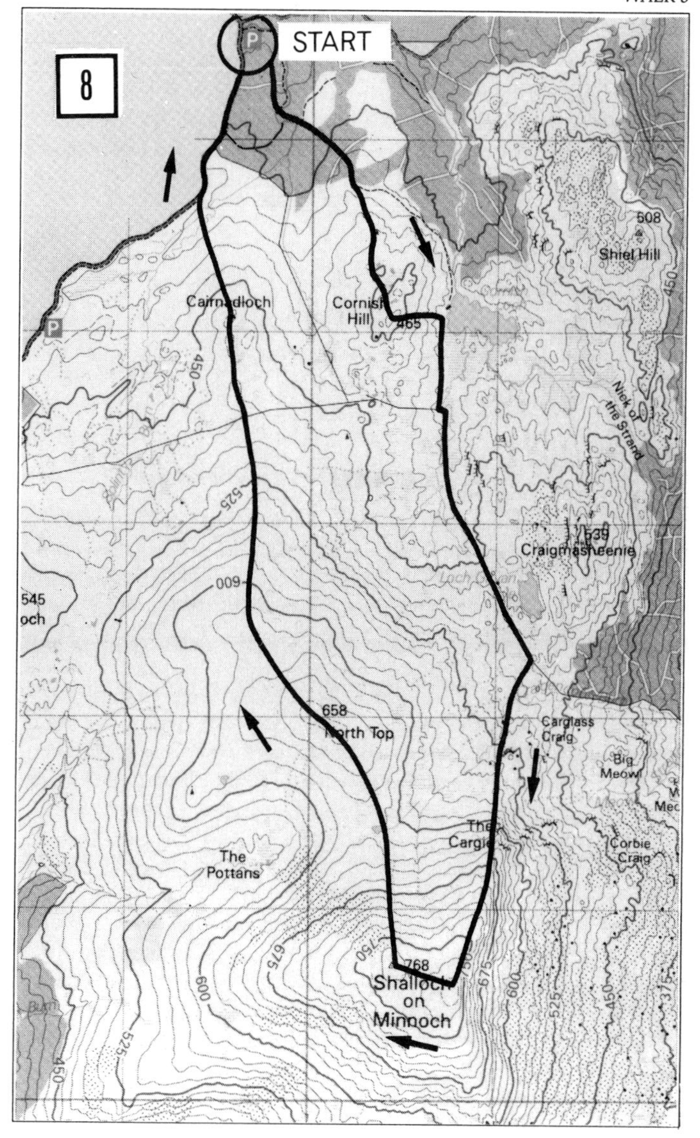
8
START
Cairnadloch
Cornish Hill
465
508
Shiel Hill
450
Nick of the Strand
525
539
Craigmasheenie
600
545
658
North Top
Carglass Craig
Big Meowl
The Cargie
Corbie Craig
The Pottans
675
750
768
Shalloch on Minnoch
600
525
450
375

forest and starts climbing the rugged slopes of Cornish Hill. There are odd boggy patches to pick your way around, but the climb is short and clear and leads up to a broad, hummocky summit bearing pools of water and finally peaking at 465m.

Follow the waymark posts over the hill and down a rugged slope of grass, rock and heather, then head southwards by turning right before reaching the shore of Cornish Loch. Stay low in the boggy valley near the loch and pick up the remains of an old fence as a guide towards a newer post and wire fence. You'll reach the fence near a corner and you should go round the corner, crossing tall, tussocky grass. Follow the fence faithfully up the broad valley. There is an abundance of tall grass and squelchy bog, with heather becoming more dominant as height is gained. You cross the infant Water of Girvan twice, and if you look to the left later you should catch a glimpse of Loch Girvan Eye on the rugged slopes of Craigmasheenie. Eventually, the fence leads onto a broad, boggy gap amid outcrops of rock.

Head off to the right, away from the fence, to face the immense bulk of Shalloch on Minnoch, looking carefully for a line to its summit. There's a rock excrescence ahead and it's best to keep to the right of it. Above that is a very steep, rocky ridge called The Cargie, which you'll need to avoid. Just to the right of The Cargie you'll notice a steep, grassy ramp, and this is the key to the best ascent. As you struggle up this steep climb, keep looking ahead and you'll eventually find that the gradient eases. A simple walk over short grass finally leads onto the broad summit area. Shalloch on Minnoch has two broad summits and if you swing to the right, you'll reach the one which has a crude shelter cairn and a trig point at 768m.

Head roughly northwards to leave the top of Shalloch on Minnoch. A steep slope which is grassy and stony in places leads down to a broad, squelchy moorland gap. There's a lochan in the gap, and by keeping to the right side of it you can make use of a vague path which runs up the slopes of North Top. There's a large rock on the ascent and you should bear slightly left at that point to cross the broad crest of North Top. There's only a tiny cairn marking the 658m summit. Keep an eye on the narrow path, which leads gently downhill on the broad moorland crest. As it swings gradually northwards, a slightly steeper and more rugged slope leads down to a broad gap where a fence has to be crossed. Keep heading northwards along the hummocky crest of Cairnadloch, which has some boggy patches. The path continues downhill towards the Glentrool Village to Straiton road, but eventually loses itself on a rugged, heathery slope. There's a small burn to be crossed before you can climb up onto the minor road, then simply follow the road into the forest to return to the car park above Stinchar Bridge.

* * *

WALK 9: CARRICK FOREST DRIVE AND CORNISH HILL

The Cornish Hill Walk is a waymarked trail from Stinchar Bridge which offers a pleasant little rugged circuit for anyone who doesn't want to grapple with the bigger and more remote Galloway Hills. It is, however, only a short circuit. The walk offered below is a longer circuit, using forest roads to make most of the distance initially, then climbing over a rugged, boggy gap before heading for Cornish Hill. The waymarked trail leading off the hill is used to return walkers to Stinchar Bridge. You could attempt this walk from car parks at either Stinchar Bridge or Loch Bradan. You could also complete the circuit using the Tunskeen Bothy as a base, with a short extension to the route alongside the nearby forest.

The Route

Distance: An 8 mile (13km) walk which starts easy and gets harder.

Start: At Stinchar Bridge - 397957.

Parking: At the car park just above Stinchar Bridge.

Starting from the car park just above Stinchar Bridge, follow the narrow tarmac forest road towards Loch Bradan. This is open to vehicles travelling both ways, so take care. You don't go all the way to the Loch Bradan car park and picnic site, but turn left to gain access to the Carrick Forest Drive. This is supposed to be one-way for vehicles, with cars supposedly barred from entering at this end. In theory, traffic should be coming towards you on the Forest Drive, but sometimes someone comes in from behind! The Forest Drive runs downhill towards some forestry buildings. You might notice a path waymarked with yellow posts which leads off to Loch

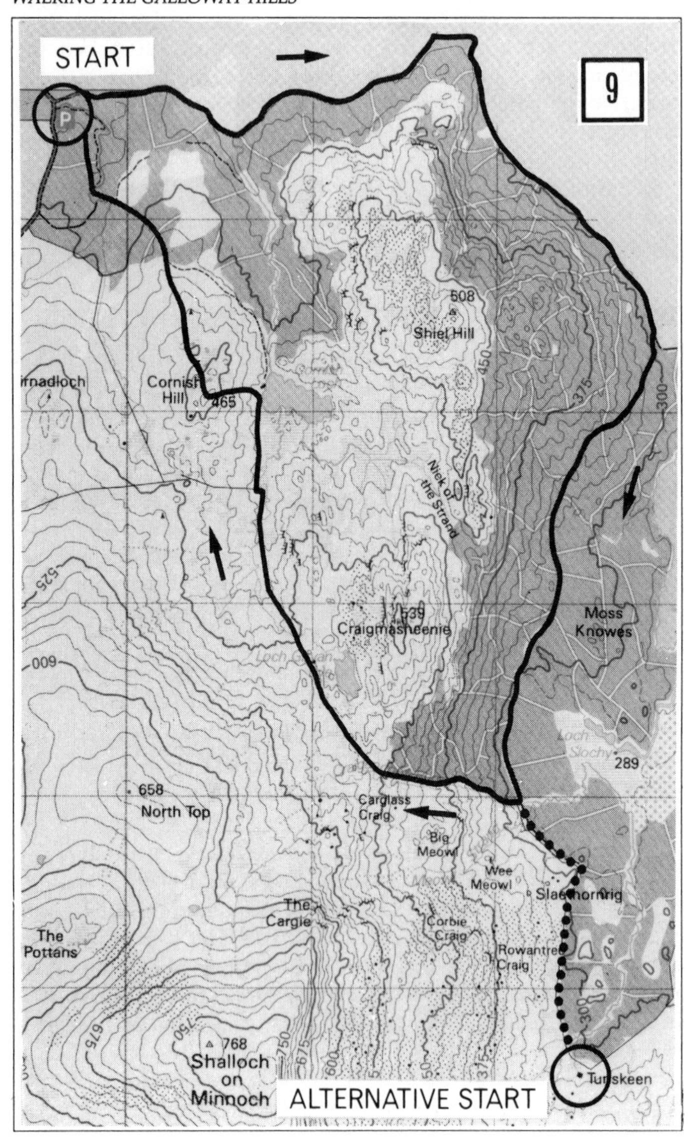
START
9
508
Shiel Hill
Cornish Hill
465
Nick of the Strand
539
Craigmasheenie
Moss Knowes
289
658
North Top
Carglass Craig
Big Meowl
Wee Meowl
Slaethornrig
The Cargie
Corbie Craig
Rowantree Craig
The Pottans
768
Shalloch on Minnoch
ALTERNATIVE START

Brecbowie - something to bear in mind for a future visit. Follow the Carrick Forest Drive until there's another forest road going off to the right. This should be followed uphill a short way, then downhill at a very gentle gradient until it emerges from the trees at Craigendoof Burn.

There's a forest road bridge over the burn at this point, but you don't actually cross it. Instead, turn right and follow the burn upstream, walking on the rough strip of ground between the burn and the forest fence. The ascent is quite difficult, running into tall bracken before long, with rocky ground encountered at a higher level. If you've time, then you can have a look at small waterfalls in Craigendoof Burn. The fence eventually strikes away from the edge of the forest and leads to a broad, boggy gap amid outcrops of rock. Keep following the fence as it offers a sure guide across difficult ground leading down from the gap. Look out on the right for a glimpse of Loch Girvan Eye on the rugged slopes of Craigmasheenie, then cross the infant Water of Girvan twice. The heather cover thins, to be replaced by tall grass and squelchy bog. The fence suddenly turns a corner where there is some tough, tussocky grass, and once round the corner you should look for the remains of an old fence branching off to the right. These remains lead along a broad, boggy valley northwards towards the shore of Cornish Loch.

As you near Cornish Loch you'll notice marker posts topped with white paint. Turn left to follow these up the rugged, grass, rock and heather slopes of Cornish Hill. A broad, hummocky summit area is reached which bears pools of water and peaks at 465m. Follow the waymark posts over the hill for the final descent, picking your way round odd boggy patches on the way. The gradient eases as the path enters a forest and runs down to cross the River Stinchar using a footbridge near the ruins of Craiglure Lodge. There's a short uphill pull, where the path has been recently realigned and in parts surfaced with wood chippings. The path swings to the right and wanders gently down through the forest to cross the River Stinchar at another footbridge. A short climb leads up to the road you started walking along earlier in the day and the car park is straight ahead.

The Carrick Forest Drive

As far as motorists are concerned, the Carrick Forest Drive is a one-way journey - from the head of Loch Doon to the head of Loch Bradan. Once you reach Loch Bradan, a tarmac road replaces the gravel forest road and you can continue to Stinchar Bridge and the Glentrool Village to Straiton road. There's a "pay & display" machine at the head of Loch Doon and you need to collect a ticket at that point in order to use the road. In practice, some motorists drive the wrong way and don't bother to pick up a ticket. There are small car parks or lay-bys beside the Forest Drive, with access to some of the walks in this guide, but space is limited and you must be careful not to block access for forestry vehicles, which need to use the roads at all times and in both directions.

* * *

WALK 10: LOCH RIECAWR AND TUNSKEEN BOTHY

Loch Riecawr is entirely surrounded by forestry plantations, but it can be viewed briefly from parts of the Carrick Forest Drive. There's a small car park, picnic table and viewpoint on the road which overlooks Loch Riecawr. If you approach this point by car, be sure to identify it promptly as you shouldn't really drive back if you overshoot it by any distance. There are two dead-end forest roads which lead southwards from the Forest Drive, and these almost entirely encircle Loch Riecawr. You can forge a link between the two roads by following forest rides to the edge of the forest and making a difficult moorland walk around the edge of the forest. The simple bothy at Tunskeen marks the turning point. It's also possible to use the outward leg of this walk as a way of reaching the bothy, then basing yourself there for a couple of days to enjoy walks into the wild heartlands of the Galloway Hills. Alternatively, if you're already based at the bothy, but find that poor weather keeps you off the big hills, then you might find some consolation in walking this low-level circuit instead.

The Route

Distance: Mostly an easy 8½ miles (14km) walk with one hard stretch.

Start: At a viewpoint on the Carrick Forest Drive - 436941.

Parking: Small parking space at the viewpoint.

Drive along the Carrick Forest Drive in the approved direction -

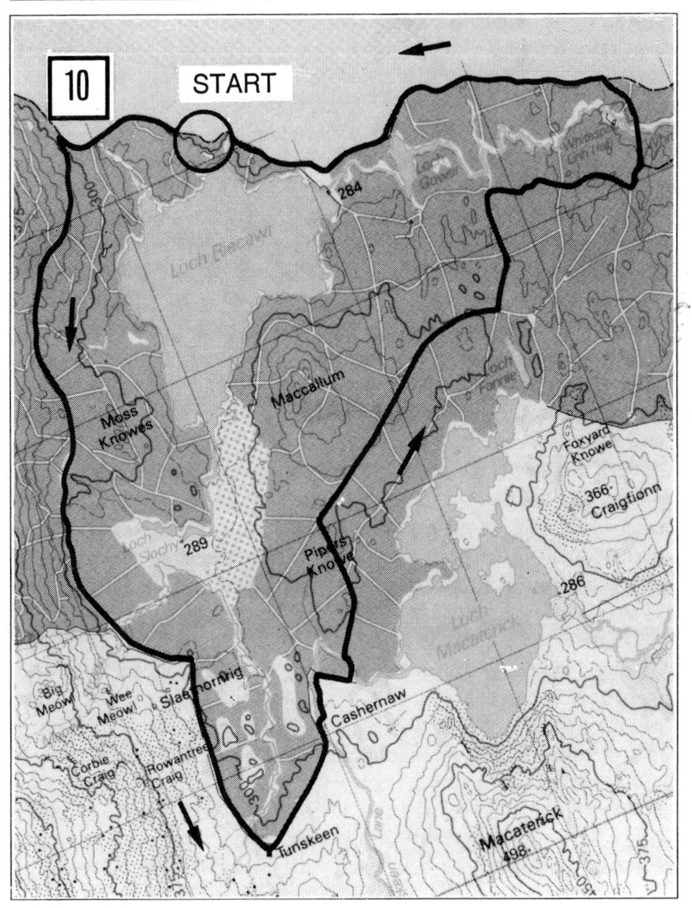

from Loch Doon towards Loch Bradan. There's a small parking space by a picnic table overlooking Loch Riecawr. Start walking by following the Forest Drive gently downhill, as if you were continuing to Loch Bradan on foot. There's a forest road branching off the Forest Drive on the left, and you follow this uphill a short way, before going downhill at a very gentle gradient until it emerges from the trees at Craigendoof Burn. The forest road is almost grass-grown at this point, and flanked by bog myrtle. Continue to the very end of the road near the ruined farmstead of Slaethornrig. There's usually a pile of logs at the end of the road and you're welcome to carry one to the Tunskeen Bothy for fuel. The bothy is reached by following a squelchy path alongside the edge of the forest. This is vegetated with tussocky grass, heather and bog myrtle. Be careful not to trip over loose fencing wire in the undergrowth. The Tunskeen Bothy stands a little way back from the forest edge, with only its roof usually visible above masses of nettles and rosebay willowherb. You might like to break there for lunch, or make use of the shelter it offers in nasty weather.

Leave the bothy and continue along the edge of the forest. Again, watch out for loose fencing wire in the grass and heather. You'll soon find yourself walking alongside Tunskeen Lane. You could follow the course of the river into the forest, but if you can cross it near Cashernaw you should do that instead. Cashernaw is a hump of rock which hides a small emergency shelter. Head back towards the edge of the forest and turn right to follow it to the point where Tunskeen Lane exits from the forest. Cross the river again and walk a short way upstream, into the forest. Turn right and follow the first forest ride you reach. This is difficult to follow as it bears long grass and bog myrtle, but it gets easier and even boasts a faint path which finally leads to the end of a forest road at Pipers Knowe.

Simply turn right and follow the forest road for much easier walking. This runs close to the shore of Loch Macaterick, but you'll catch hardly a glimpse of it between the trees. There is a short, trodden path on the right which you could use to approach the little Loch Fannie, but otherwise you should stay on the broad forest road. The road turns around numerous corners, but you only need to remember to turn left at a junction of forest roads and follow the road which crosses Whitespout Lane. You could wander a short way upstream to see the waterfall of Whitespout Linn, otherwise follow the forest road uphill a short way and turn left along the Carrick Forest Drive. The Forest Drive is fairly level at first, then there's a roadside bench overlooking the little Loch Gower. You'll catch a glimpse of the dam of Loch Riecawr before the Forest Drive climbs gently uphill to return you to the viewpoint and car park where you started the walk, overlooking Loch Riecawr.

Loch Riecawr

Loch Riecawr is actually a reservoir with a dam holding the water in check. The flow of water along Whitespout Lane from Loch Riecawr to Loch Doon can be regulated so that the level of Loch Doon can be topped up from time to time. Water is drawn off from Loch Doon to boost the flow of water in the Water of Deugh, where power is generated at a hydro-electric plant. Apart from providing the head of water which ultimately produces electricity, Loch Riecawr is also popular with fishermen who have easy access to its shores from the Carrick Forest Drive. There is also a small fishing lodge.

* * *

WALK 11: KIRRIEREOCH HILL FROM TUNSKEEN BOTHY

Despite its limitations, the Tunskeen Bothy makes a good base from which to explore the wilder parts of the Galloway Hills. Once you're in occupation you've no need to endure lengthy walk-ins before getting to grips with the more remote hills. Obviously, you've got to carry all your supplies in with you, but you could probably leave most of it safely at the bothy and travel light on the hills each day. There's a rugged circuit which keeps high on the hills above the Tunskeen Bothy, occasionally offering a view of this tiny hut and making you realise how remote its surroundings really are. The main hills on this circuit are Macaterick, Kirriereoch Hill, Tarfessock and Shalloch on Minnoch. You can cut the walk short by omitting Shallock on Minnoch and making a direct descent to the bothy at the end of the day.

The Route

Distance: A difficult hill walk of 9 miles (15km).

Start: At Tunskeen Bothy - 425905.

Parking: Use the Loch Bradan car park for overnight parking.

Walk eastwards from the Tunskeen Bothy, across tussocky grass, heather and bog myrtle. Cross Tunskeen Lane and start the gradual ascent of Macaterick. It's heavy going underfoot, but maybe the easiest course is to aim for a point on the ridge to the north of the summit, then turn right to follow the broad, rugged ridge to the top of the hill. There are fine views over the convoluted shore of Loch

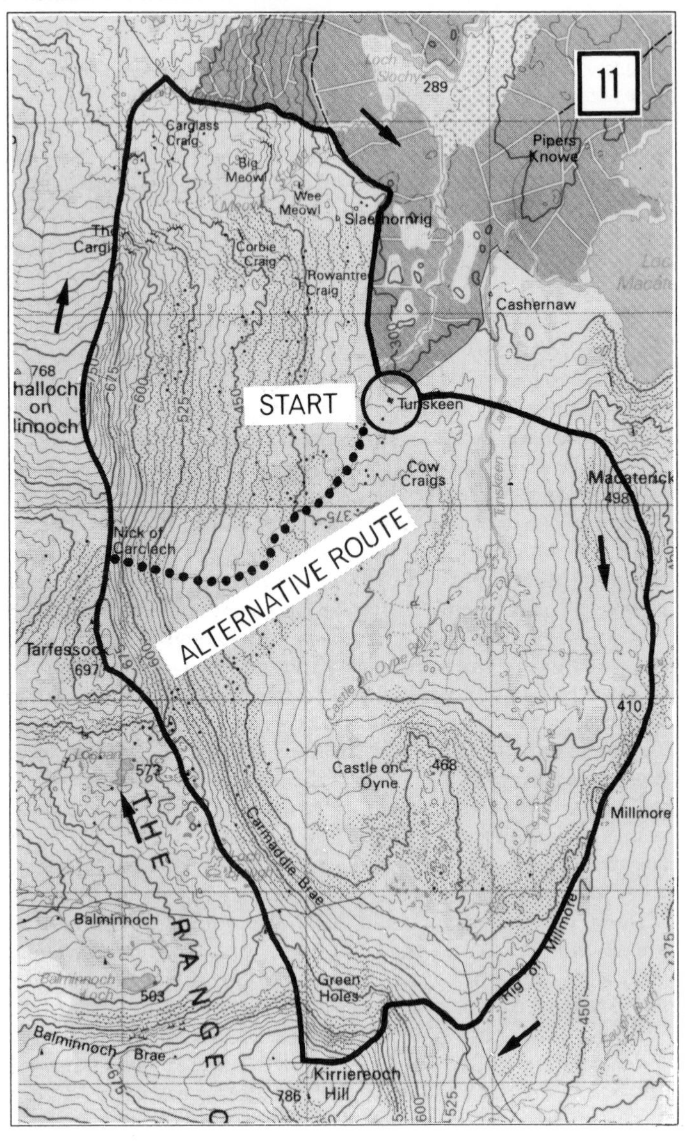
11
START
ALTERNATIVE ROUTE
Carglass Craig
Big Meowl
Wee Meowl
Slaethornrig
Corbie Craig
Rowantree Craig
Pipers Knowe
Cashernaw
Tunskeen
Cow Craigs
Macaterick
498
Nick of Carclach
Tarfessock
697
Castle on Oyne
468
410
Millmore
Rig of Millmore
Carmaddie Brae
Green Holes
Kirriereoch Hill
786
Balminnoch
Balminnoch Brae
503
573
THE RANGE
768
Shalloch on Minnoch
289

Macaterick, as well as the more distant forested shore of Loch Riecawr. In all other directions are rugged ranges of hills. The 498m summit of Macaterick has a cairn and there is plenty of granite exposed in the heather and grass.

Follow the broad crest roughly southwards from Macaterick. There's only the vaguest trace of a trodden path which passes outcrops of rock, boggy patches and occasional areas of bilberry amid the grass and heather. There are odd humps of granite - such as the top of Millmore on the broad crest. After crossing the next hump and following the Rig of Millmore, there are huge boulders scattered over the squelchy ground, but no real outcrops of rock. The Rig of Millmore begins to steepen and there's a fence to cross. A ruined wall is encountered a little higher up the slope and you turn right to follow this uphill. The wall zig-zags up the steep slopes of Kirriereoch Hill and eventually levels out on a broad area of stony ground and short grass. You could detour to the 786m summit, but there are two cairns - one small one on the very top of the hill and a larger one off to one side which has been made into a small shelter.

Return to the ruined wall and cross over it to start descending the steep, stony northern face of Kirriereoch Hill. The ground begins to level out and you cross a fence and pass the little Loch Brough. Ahead is a broad, hummocky, lochan-strewn gap which could be a problem to walk across in poor visibility. In fine weather, however, you can enjoy the views over the Carmaddie Brae into the wild heartlands of the Galloway Hills. At the end of the broad gap there's a short, rugged climb uphill to the 697m summit of Tarfessock. There is a cairn on top of a low, rocky outcrop. Simply walk straight past the cairn and around small outcrops of rock, following a vague path along the broad ridge leading down to the Nick of Carclach. A boulder sits on the gap at that point. You have the option of cutting the walk short by heading straight down the rugged slope from the gap and walking across a boulder-strewn moorland to return to the Tunskeen Bothy. You would roughly trace the course of a small burn across tussocky grass, heather and boulders before aiming towards the bothy.

The walk can be continued over Shalloch on Minnoch as follows. A vague path rises from the Nick of Carclach, but is soon lost on the broad slopes of Shalloch on Minnoch. The grass underfoot is short

The view from the bouldery Millmore to Macaterick

and there is a thin scattering of boulders. A small cairn sits on top of a broad rise, or you could detour to an adjacent rise to visit the 768m trig point and a cairn which has been fashioned into a windbreak. If you go to the trig point, make sure you return to the first broad rise to start the descent from Shalloch on Minnoch. Walk roughly northwards along a broad, easy ridge. As this steepens, keep somewhat to the left side of the ridge to avoid the steep, rocky end of The Cargie. Aim to use a steep ramp of grass to one side of the rocky ridge. The lower slopes are quite rugged and you should keep to the left of a rocky excrescence on the way to a broad, boggy gap amid outcrops of rock. Cross over Craigendoof Burn to reach a fence on this gap, then turn right.

Follow the fence faithfully downhill, staying on the strip of rough ground between the forest fence and the burn. There's some rocky ground to cross on the descent, then you'll run into tall bracken later. If you've time, then look out for lovely little waterfalls in the burn. Eventually, you'll land on a forest road and by turning right you can follow the road to its very end near the ruined farmstead of Slaethornrig. There's usually a pile of logs at the end of the road and you're welcome to carry one to the Tunskeen Bothy for fuel. The bothy is reached by following a squelchy path alongside the edge of the forest. This is vegetated with tussocky grass, heather and bog myrtle. Be careful not to trip over loose fencing wire in the undergrowth. The Tunskeen Bothy stands a little way back from the forest edge, with only its roof usually visible above masses of nettles and rosebay willowherb.

The Tunskeen Bothy

The Tunskeen Bothy is a very simple, single-roomed bothy which is only just weathertight. It was never more than a simple shepherd's dwelling and isn't suitable for more than a handful of walkers. In past years its roof has been blown off a couple of times by strong gales. There is a stove inside, but you need to carry in sawn logs from a pile dumped at the end of the forest road at Slaethornrig. You'll need to bring a saw and an axe to deal with the logs. There are gaps around the bothy, so wind and rain can get in from some quarters, as well as midges in the summer months, so be prepared for some discomfort. Not far from Tunskeen, hidden behind a rock near Tunskeen Lane, is the former Cashernaw Bothy. This was a very simple dwelling which fell completely ruinous. However, it has been made into a tiny, low-roofed shelter which could accommodate a couple of bodies in some discomfort. You probably wouldn't choose to spend a night there normally, but bear the place in mind in case emergency accommodation is needed in that area.

* * *

WALK 12: MULLWHARCHAR FROM TUNSKEEN BOTHY

If you're prepared to use the Tunskeen Bothy as a base, then you can have easier access to the wilder parts of the Galloway Hills. Macaterick is only a short walk away from the door of the bothy, and once you're on top of the hill you can look round at a range of higher hills separated by rugged gaps or broad, bleak, boggy valleys. You could walk all the way round the valley of Eglin Lane, staying on high hills and visiting Macaterick at both the beginning and end of the walk. If would be a long walk-in from the nearest road to complete such a round and you'd have to endure being in the forest for quite some time. Starting and finishing at the Tunskeen Bothy means you don't have to spend any time in the forest. If you start

Mullwharchar rises above the waters of Loch Enoch

early and finish late, then you could add an ascent of Merrick as an "extra", though the ground underfoot is rough enough and you may find that there just isn't time for a summit bid. The huge, bouldery dome of Mullwharchar is therefore the highest hill covered on this round - a noble and remote height which doesn't see too many walkers.

The Route

Distance: A difficult hill walk of 10 miles (16km).

Start: At Tunskeen Bothy - 425905.

Parking: Use the Loch Bradan car park for overnight parking.

Walk eastwards from the Tunskeen Bothy, across tussocky grass, heather and bog myrtle. Cross Tunskeen Lane and start the gradual ascent of Macaterick. It's heavy going underfoot, but maybe the easiest course is to aim for a point on the ridge to the north of the summit, then turn right to follow the broad, rugged ridge to the top of the hill. There are fine views over the convoluted shore of Loch Macaterick, as well as the more distant forested shore of Loch

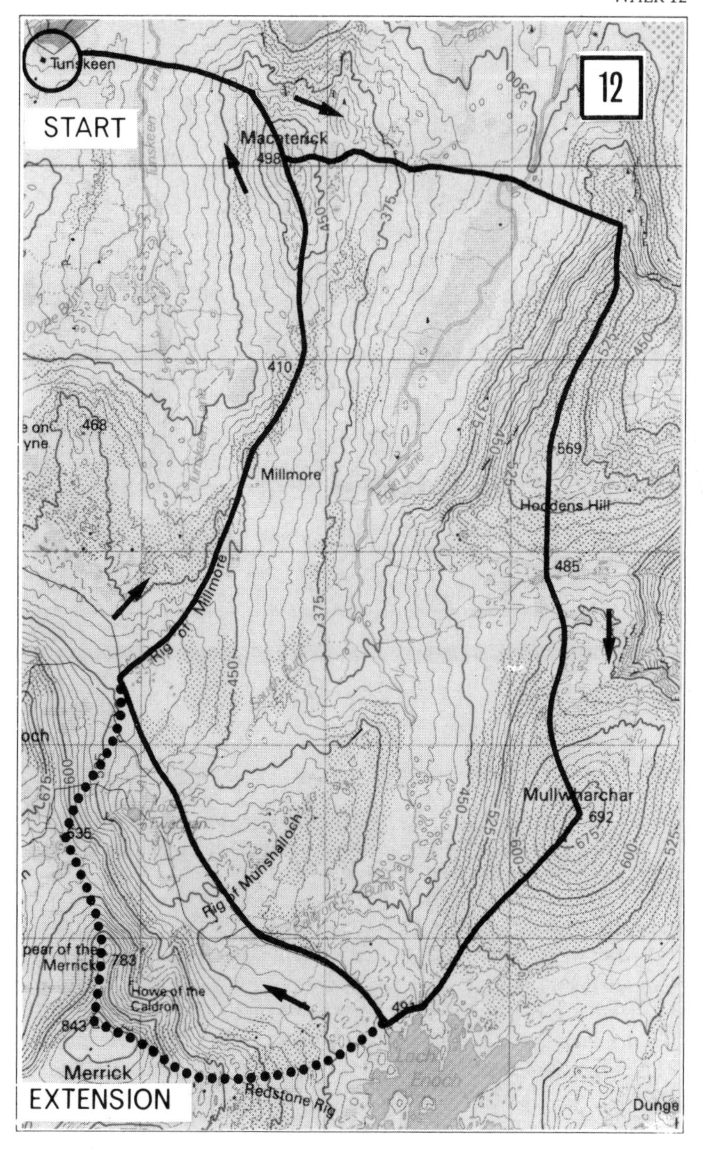
12
START
Tunskeen
Macaterick
498
410
468
Millmore
Rig of Millmore
375
450
569
Hoodens Hill
485
Mullwharchar
692
Rig of Munshalloch
635
Spear of the Merrick
783
Howe of the Caldron
843
Merrick
Redstone Rig
EXTENSION
Dunge

Riecawr. In all other directions are rugged ranges of hills. The 498m summit of Macaterick has a cairn and there is plenty of granite exposed in the heather and grass.

Descend towards Eglin Lane, picking a careful way down the rugged slope, making detours around outcropping rock. The tough vegetation cover makes for a difficult descent, then there's a walk across the broad, boggy base of the valley, crossing tussocky grass. Find a place to cross Eglin Lane, then climb up the rugged slope beyond, which is composed of grass, heather and rock. it's hard work, but things become easier when you reach the crest of the ridge. Turn right to follow the rugged ridge to the top of Hoodens Hill. There is a path which has been marked by small cairns and this climbs up to the broad, rocky crest of the hill. The summit ridge is almost level, but finally peaks at 569m and bears a cairn. There's no real path trodden further southwards down to a broad gap, but it's simply a case of walking down a very rugged slope pitched at a fairly gentle gradient. Cross the gap by walking between two small lochans sitting on the gap, then climb up the broad, grassy, rocky slopes of Mullwharchar. Again, there is no path on the ground, so you have to pick a way to the top around boggy and rocky areas. There's a summit cairn at 692m and views towards the great granite mass of the Dungeon Hills further to the south.

Head south-westwards from the top of Mullwharchar to descend grassy, bouldery slopes to reach the hummocky ground on the northern shore of Loch Enoch. Most of the way down you'll have a view of the amazing shoreline of the loch, with all its tiny bays and headlands, as well as little islets and rocks which peep above the surface of the water. Cross over the infant Eglin Lane which exits from the loch, then continue around the shore a short way to find a fence and ruined wall. Turn right to follow the fence away from the loch, crossing broad, rugged slopes which lead up towards the top of Merrick. (An ascent of Merrick is something you might consider as an "extra".) The fence goes across the headwaters of Caldron Burn and crosses the broad rise of the Rig of Munshalloch, before passing below the little Loch Twachan and climbing gently onto the Rig of Millmore.

Descending towards the Spear of the Merrick

Corserine as seen from the top of Kirriereoch Hill
Looking along Tunskeen Lane to Macaterick

Turn right to branch away from the fence, walking down the broad, boggy, boulder-strewn Rig of Millmore. There's a hump to cross, then the next hump is of granite and this is Millmore itself. The ascent of Macaterick along the broad crest is fairly gently graded, but the ground is quite rugged. There are patches of bog in the grass and heather, and you'll need to pick a way around outcrops or rock, passing occasional patches of bilberry before reaching the summit cairn at 498m. To end the walk, you should walk down the ridge you climbed earlier in the day, then head off to the left to cross Tunskeen Lane to return to the Tunskeen Bothy. In clear weather it seems very insignificant surrounded as it is on all sides by huge hills, but in foul weather you'd be glad of what little shelter it offers for the night.

Mullwharchar

Mullwharchar is an enormous, boulder-strewn dome of granite in the heart of the Galloway Hills. Few tread on its pathless slopes, but in the mid-1980s it was mentioned several times in the media. The hill, being a fairly stable mass of granite, had been shortlisted as a possible site for the deep storage of spent nuclear fuel. Other sites around Britain were also being considered - usually in remote and unpopulated areas. However, there was a concerted campaign against each and every one of the proposed dump sites. The search for a "suitable" site continued, and ultimately attention was focused on the already much-abused Sellafield site on the Cumbria coast.

Loch Enoch

Loch Enoch has an amazing amoeboid shape, spreading arms of water across a barren, boulder-strewn gap in the hills. Numerous bays and headlands are apparent in views from the surrounding hills and one feature to look for is the "Loch-in-Loch". Look carefully at the largest islet in the loch, then look for the tiny pool of water sitting on it! Some of the bays on Loch Enoch are flanked by beaches of coarse white sand. The sand is mainly made up of quartz grains washed from the granite, then sifted and sorted by wind and water action. It was highly prized for sharpening scythes in the past, and no doubt when Robert the Bruce was camped in the area during 1307 it may well be that the little army sharpened its swords and daggers by Loch Enoch too.

⁂ ⁂ ⁂

WALK 13: MACATERICK FROM THE CARRICK FOREST DRIVE

Macaterick is only a small hill, but it is quite rugged on all sides. There are forest roads leading towards it from the Carrick Forest Drive, but they peter out before they've even reached the edge of the forest. However, forest rides can be used to reach the surrounding moorlands, then a difficult trudge leads over the top of Macaterick. Loch Macaterick is completely encircled by this walk, though you'll only obtain a decent view of it from the top of the hill. The circuit can be completed from the Carrick Forest Drive, or you could easily adapt the walk so that it starts and finishes at the Tunskeen Bothy. You might find some consolation in a walk over Macaterick when cloud covers the high hills all round.

The Route

Distance: A 7½ mile (12km) walk varying from easy to difficult.

Start: On the Carrick Forest Drive near Whitespout Linn - 457935.

Parking: Close to a junction on the Forest Drive near Whitespout Linn.

Park off the side of the Carrick Forest Drive at a point where a forest road leads down towards Whitespout Lane, near Whitespout Linn. Walk down the forest road to cross the river, then head uphill and turn left along another forest road. This road suddenly turns right and climbs gently uphill, crossing the broad rise of Wee Craigfionn. As soon as the road starts running downhill, turn left and walk along a forest ride. There is a narrow path trodden along this ride, but also plenty of long grass and some bog myrtle. The ride suddenly runs down to a footbridge crossing a rocky gorge on Eglin Lane.

Don't cross the footbridge, but turn right and follow Eglin Lane upstream, walking on the rough strip of ground between the river and the edge of the forest. There is tussocky grass, bog myrtle and some squelchy areas to negotiate, even beyond the edge of the forest and further upstream to where the tributary of Black Garpel flows into Eglin Lane. Cross over Black Garpel to reach a low, hummocky, boggy moorland, noting a nearby sheepfold near the confluence of the two rivers. Macaterick rises above the broad, lower ground and the walk towards it is quite difficult. The whole flank of the hill is

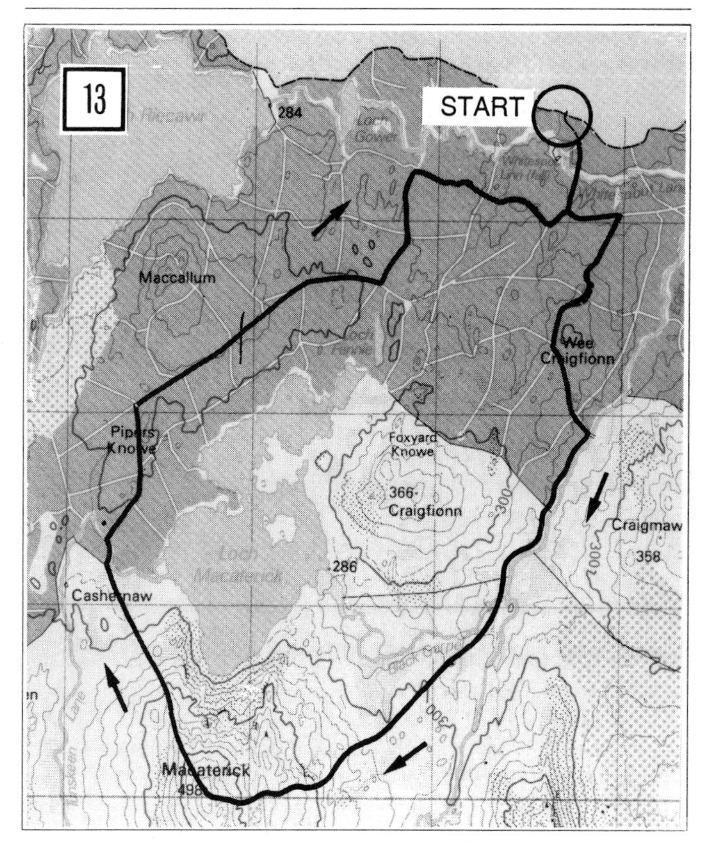

rocky, with heather and tussocky grass. You'll probably find it best to zig-zag between the rocky outcrops using vegetated strips between them. At length, the 498m summit cairn is reached in an area where plenty of granite is exposed in the grass and heather. There are views over the convoluted shore of Loch Macaterick, as well as a more distant view of the forested shore of Loch Riecawr. In all other directions are rugged ranges of hills.

Descend roughly north-westwards to pick up the rugged ridge running down towards Cashernaw. The descent is fairly easy for a short way, but becomes more difficult. There are a few outcrops of rock to detour around, then there's a walk across a level moorland at the bottom where tussocky grass makes for slow progress. You should aim for the point where Tunskeen Lane flows out of the forest before flowing into Loch Macaterick. Cross over Tunskeen Lane as you trace it into the forest. Turn right to follow the first forest ride you reach. This is difficult to follow as it bears long grass and bog myrtle, but it gets easier and even boasts a faint path which finally leads to the end of a forest road at Pipers Knowe. Simply turn right and follow the forest road for much easier walking. This runs close to the shore of Loch Macaterick, but you'll catch hardly a glimpse of it between the trees. There is a short, trodden path on the right which you could use to approach the little Loch Fannie, but otherwise you should stay on the broad forest road. The road turns around numerous corners, but you only need to remember to turn left at a junction of forest roads and follow the road which crosses Whitespout Lane. You could wander a short way upstream to see the waterfall of Whitespout Linn, otherwise follow the forest road uphill a short way to return to the Carrick Forest Drive where you started.

Macaterick

Along with the Faas and the Marshalls, the Macatericks were a wild and unruly gypsy clan who lived in and around the Galloway Hills. They kept on the move and established only semi-permanent dwellings, though sometimes they led a more settled life. They frequented any fairs and gatherings in the area, but also considered it fair to take anything they fancied from their neighbours - and they were able to defend their ill-gotten gains with considerable ferocity. S.R.Crockett's novel The Raiders *weaves fact with fiction to present a tale of these wild folk. Cave Macaterick is described as being some distance up the slopes of Macaterick from the confluence of Black Garpel and Eglin Lane. Some say that the entrance to this hideaway has collapsed, while others doubt whether it ever existed. These days, Macaterick is the name for a rugged little hill in the heart of the Galloway Hills, but it's also a local name for the swarms of midges which rise from the bogs each summer and draw blood from visiting walkers!*

* * *

WALK 14: AROUND CRAIGMAWHANNAL FROM LOCH DOON

Loch Doon is a popular place and many people drive along its shores looking for a place to picnic or fish. Some simply park the car and set off for a short stroll, while others have their sights set on more distant objectives. The walk described below offers a fairly simple circuit around the forested slopes of Craigmawhannal, with glimpses of the higher hills between the trees. The walk is mostly along broad, firm forest roads and includes a stretch of the Carrick Forest Drive. Major rivers which are crossed include Gala Lane, Eglin Lane and Carrick Lane, and unusually there are footbridges and road bridges so you won't have to look for places offering safe fords. There is a stretch of more difficult moorland walking close to the summit of Craigmawhannal. There should be enough time before or after this walk to have a look at the remains of Loch Doon Castle, or break for a snack at Craigmalloch Cottage, or you could finish the day with a run along the Carrick Forest Drive. This is a suitable walk to consider when clouds lay low on the higher hills, and it should familiarise you with some of the access points for reaching the wilder hills beyond.

The Route

Distance: A 8½ mile (14km) walk which is mostly easy.

Start: At a bridge over Carrick Lane - 476942.

Parking: Near the bridge over Carrick Lane.

A minor road runs alongside Loch Doon and continues as the Carrick Forest Drive at a "pay & display" machine. Don't go along the Forest Drive, but turn off to the left and park near a bridge over Carrick Lane. Cross the bridge on foot and follow the rough road uphill to pass Starr Cottage. The road runs down to cross another bridge - this one spanning a rocky gorge over Gala Lane. Both Carrick Lane and Gala Lane flow into Loch Doon after passing these bridges. As soon as you've crossed Gala Lane, turn right along a forest road which usually has a gate across it. The road is generally level and you simply follow it to its very end.

A path continues from the end of the road, going gently down through a younger plantation to reach a footbridge over Gala Lane.

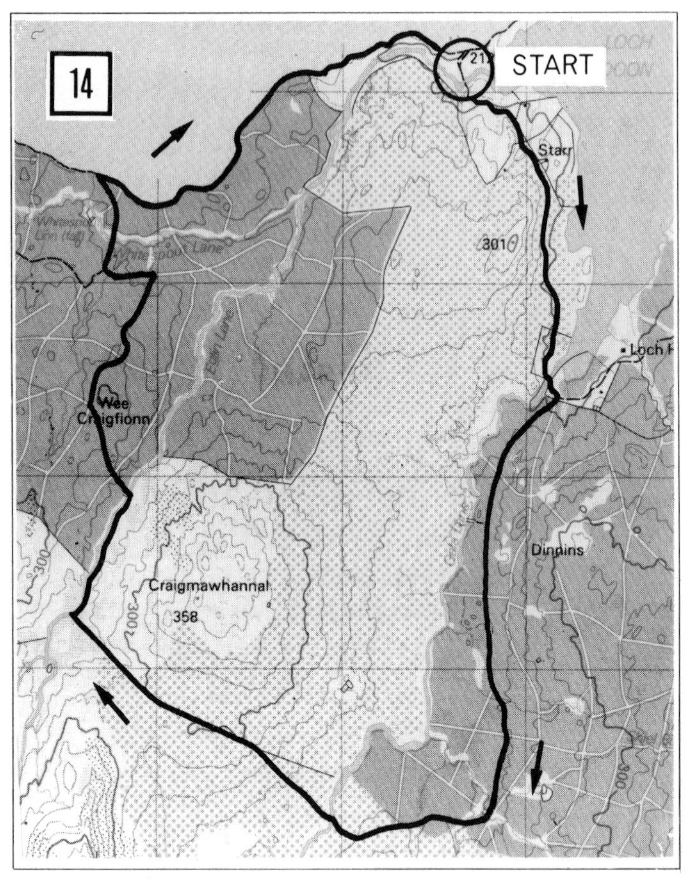

The bridge makes use of a natural crossing point and there's a view of the rocky flanks of the Dungeon Hills upstream. The path continues up a forest ride and eventually runs alongside a fence to cross the broad shoulder of Craigmawhannal. You don't go to the 358m summit, but follow the fence downhill to leave the forest. There's very little trace of a path by the fence at this point and the ground is covered in tussocky grass with some boggy bits. You need to cross the fence when you reach the banks of Eglin Lane, then follow the river downstream. There is a very narrow path which might be of some use, but it runs through tall grass and bog myrtle and can be difficult to trace. Continue downstream until you reach a footbridge spanning a rocky gorge.

Cross the footbridge carefully, as it is a bit wobbly, then walk up a steep forest ride. There is a narrow path along the ride, but there's plenty of long grass and bog myrtle too. The forest ride runs into a forest road, which you follow by turning right and crossing the broad rise of Wee Craigfionn. After going gently downhill, the forest road suddenly turns left. Turn right at a nearby junction to follow another forest road across Whitespout Lane. You could wander a short way upstream on the river to see the waterfall of Whitespout Linn, otherwise follow the forest road uphill a short way and turn right along the Carrick Forest Drive. The drive is supposed to be one-way for vehicles and the traffic should be coming towards you, but there's always someone who comes the wrong way! Walk along the drive to emerge from the forest with a view across Carrick Lane to the Rhinns of Kells. A right turn at the "pay & display" machine leads you back down to the parking space where you started the walk.

Loch Doon Castle

Very little is known about Loch Doon Castle, but its polygonal shape and close-fitting ashlar masonry makes it very special. It was visited by Robert the Bruce, but at that time it stood where a small island now peeps above the surface of Loch Doon. the castle was removed stone by stone when the waters of the loch were being raised, and rebuilt by the shore of the reservoir. The original orientation of the castle was maintained, so its gateway now faces the hillside, whereas you might have expected it to face the other way round. The foundations of the castle can still be discerned on the little island.

Loch Doon

Loch Doon is actually a reservoir, with its dam in the direction of Dalmellington. The surface of the original loch was raised and the head of water is used to feed rivers on the opposite side of the Rhinns of Kells. A tunnel bored beneath the hills takes water from Loch Doon into Carsphairn Lane and the Water of Deugh. Power stations are strung throughout the Glenkens from Kendoon to Tongland, all using the head of water which has been captured in the Galloway Hills to generate electricity. The scheme has been running since 1936 and Tongland is geared to providing interested visitors with background information. The loch is also popular with casual visitors, picnickers, fishermen, etc. There is also the Craigmalloch Outdoor Centre, where youngsters are introduced to a range of outdoor activities in the Galloway Hills.

* * *

WALK 15: MULLWHARCHAR FROM LOCH HEAD

Mullwharchar is fairly central to the Galloway Hills and so proves to be difficult to approach. Two lines of approach using forestry roads suggest themselves - one involving a walk-in from the head of Loch Doon and the other using the Backhill of Bush Bothy as a base. Either way, you'll be in the forestry plantations for some time before reaching the open hillsides. At least the distance can be covered fairly quickly using the firm forest roads. The route offered below starts and finishes at Loch Head, near the head of Loch Doon. After the forested walk-in, the route crosses Mullwharchar and neighbouring Hoodens Hill, where the ground is really quite rugged. The start and finish of the walk are just off the map extract, but you can refer to either the previous map or the next map for the bit of the route which is missing.

The Route

Distance: A 12½ mile (20km) walk starting easy and getting harder.
Start: At the south end of Loch Doon - 482924.
Parking: Beside the forest road near Gala Lane.

A minor road runs alongside Loch Doon and continues as the Carrick Forest Drive at a "pay & display" machine. Don't go along the Forest Drive, but turn off to the left and drive across both Carrick Lane and Gala Lane using a rough forest road. Park off the road close to Gala Lane and continue on foot. Turn right to go along a forest road which usually has a gate across it. The road is generally level and you follow it as far as a prominent bend to the right. Just on the bend, before the road crosses Kirreoch Burn, is a forest ride heading off roughly southwards. Follow this ride uphill at a gentle

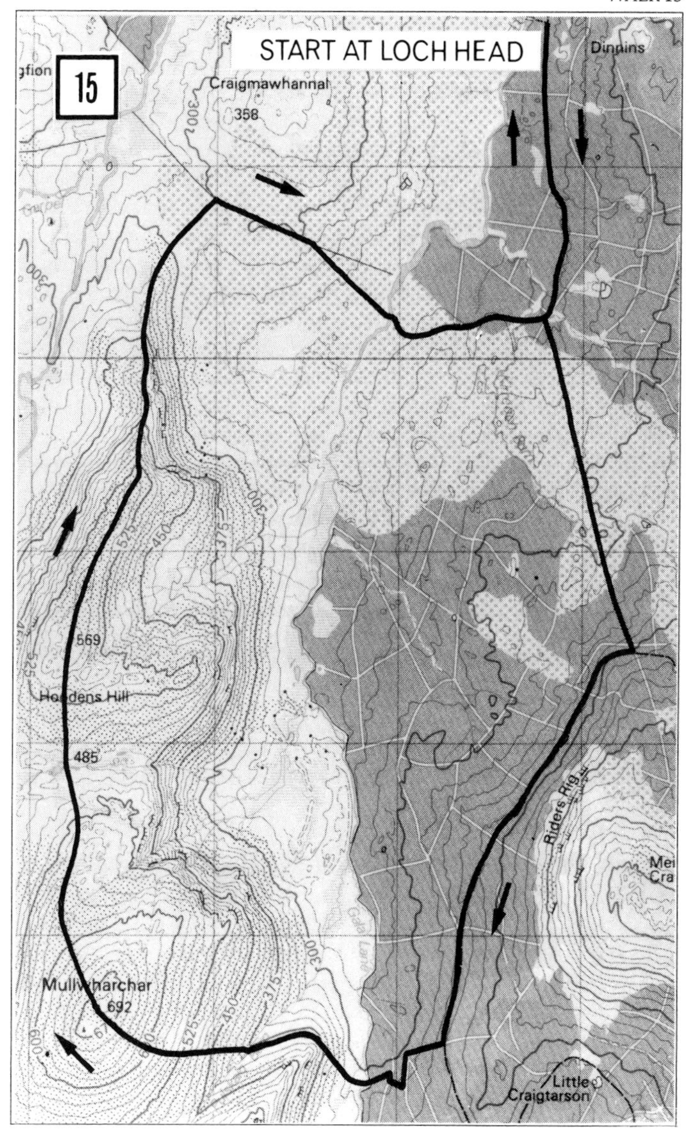
START AT LOCH HEAD
15
Dinnins
Craigmawhannal
358
300
569
Hoddens Hill
485
Mullwharchar
692
Riders Rig
Little
Craigtarson

gradient, though there is some tussocky grass and boggy areas to cross. After crossing Kirreoch Burn the gradient steepens, but the ride soon hits a forest road where there's a stout post and some fire beaters.

Turn right to walk along the forest road, which is mostly fairly level. You continue until you reach a point opposite the great bulk of Mullwharchar, then you need to watch carefully for a series of short forest rides which can be linked to take you through the trees to the open hillside. The first ride runs off to the right of the forest road, and this ride goes steeply downhill and is vegetated with grass and bog myrtle. Turn left at the bottom and follow a broader ride past a group of boulders. Continue further, looking carefully on the right for a narrow, overgrown ride which leads down to a junction of forest rides near a boulder. Behind the boulder is a short ride leading down to the forest ride and across the infant Gala Lane.

After crossing both the fence and the small burn, bear to the right to head up the rugged slopes below Brishie. A narrow path of sorts actually climbs across the slope and turns around the lower end of the ridge. With care, this path can be followed across the slope towards Pulskaig Burn, by which time it will have faded away. Once across the burn, you might as well swing round and walk straight up the rugged slopes of Mullwharchar. Grass, heather, bog and boulders cover the hill almost all the way to the summit cairn at 692m. Fine views of the surrounding hills are available throughout the ascent of Mullwharchar.

Head roughly northwards to reach Hoodens Hills. There's a descent down a rugged slope pitched at a fairly gentle gradient, then you pass between two small lochans sitting on a gap below. Climb up the broad, grassy, rocky slopes of Hoodens Hill to reach the summit cairn at 569m. Continue along the broad, rocky, almost level crest of the hill. The crest narrows to a rugged ridge as it falls, and this bears a trodden path marked by small cairns. Keep an eye peeled off to the right on the lower parts of the ridge, as you need to branch off into a young forestry plantation using a forest ride. The ride is grassy, with bog myrtle, and it runs up a gentle slope to reach a fence. Turn right to follow the fence across a broad shoulder of Craigmawhannal, but once the fence starts to descend, look out to the right for another forest ride which takes the path down towards

Gala Lane. There's a footbridge across the river which makes use of a natural crossing point, then the path climbs gently to reach the end of a forest road in a more mature plantation. The forest road soon swings round to the left and at that point you'll be following the route you walked earlier in the day. The forest road stays fairly level and leads back to the junction where you parked your car near Gala Lane.

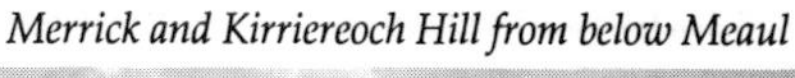

WALK 16: CARLIN'S CAIRN FROM LOCH HEAD

The Rhinns of Kells is a name which was originally applied only to part of the long range of hills extending from Loch Doon southwards to the River Dee, but these days the name is used to label the entire range. The northern end of the range offers a fairly straightforward ridge walk, though there are extensively forested slopes to be negotiated in order to create a circular walk. An approach to the hills can be made using a forest road running around the shore of Loch Doon. Four broad, grassy or stony summits can be crossed on the ridge walk, with Carlin's Cairn being the highest and final one to be

Merrick and Kirriereoch Hill from below Meaul

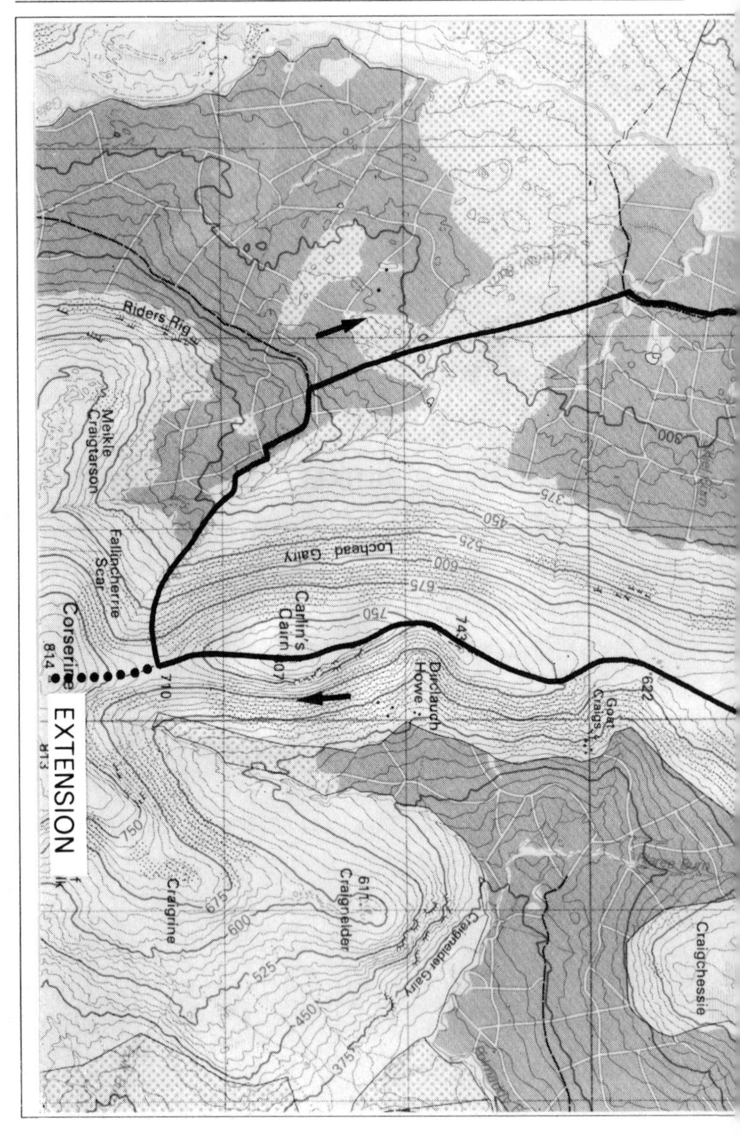
Riders Rig
Meikle Craigtarson
Fallincherrie Scar
Corserine
814
EXTENSION
710
Carlin's Cairn
807
Lochead Gairy
Dirclaugh Howe
743
Goat Craigs
622
Craignelder
611
Craigrine
Craignelder Gairy
Craigchessie

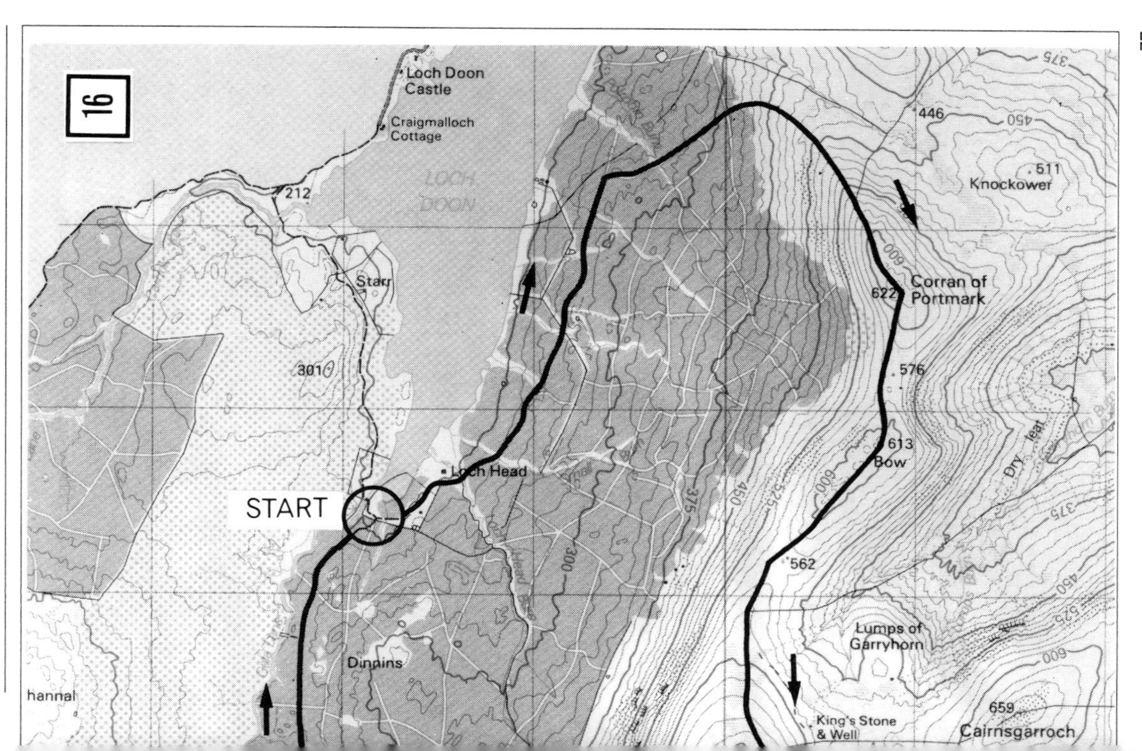
16
Loch Doon Castle
Craigmalloch Cottage
212
Starr
301
START
Loch Head
Dinnins
hannal
300
375
450
525
600
446
511
Knockower
622
Corran of Portmark
576
613
Bow
562
Dry leat
Lumps of Garryhorn
King's Stone & Well
659
Cairnsgarroch

climbed. You could, however, extend the walk to Corserine, or even continue ever-southwards to the River Dee. A descent into the forests is followed by a long walk-out to Loch Head, though you could instead descend to spend a night at the Backhill of Bush Bothy. Compared with other walks in the Galloway Hills, the walk along these hills is reasonably easy once you're clear of the forests. In clear weather there are excellent views of the surrounding country and there's less need to worry about the intricacies of route-finding along the ridge.

The Route

Distance: A long, moderate hill walk of 11 miles (18km).

Start: At the south end of Loch Doon - 482924.

Parking: Beside the forest road near Gala Lane.

A minor road runs alongside Loch Doon and continues as the Carrick Forest Drive at a "pay & display" machine. Don't go along the Forest Drive, but turn off to the left and drive across both Carrick Lane and Gala Lane using a rough forest road. Park off the road close to Gala Lane and continue on foot. The forest road runs past the nearby buildings at Loch Head and you follow the road to its very end. Tall bracken appears to bar further progress, but you'll actually find that a narrow path forges onwards through it all. Cross a small burn and keep walking along the forest ride. There is less bracken and more grass and bog myrtle. Eventually, you can branch uphill to the right along another forest ride, crossing over Polrobin Burn later. At the end of this ride, another forest ride cuts across and the way directly ahead seems barred by trees. Look carefully and you'll find that a short path runs through the trees and gives access to the open hillside beyond. As you leave the edge of the forest, swing gradually round to the right and climb up the broad, rugged slopes of Corran of Portmark. The ascent is mainly grassy, with some heather and bilberry. A fence finally leads to the 622m summit, where there is a small cairn across the fence.

You can either follow the fence from Corran of Portmark to a neighbouring summit of Bow, or follow a narrow path along the broad crest linking the two tops. The crest is broad and grassy, but there are bits of rock poking through on the ascent of Bow. The summit cairn stands at 613m. The fence now has a trodden path alongside it and it wanders gently downhill from Bow. There's another broad gap to cross, then on the next ascent a wall runs into the fence from the left. Keep following the fence uphill. You later have the option of branching away from the fence, to the right, to aim straight for the summit of Meaul. In poor visibility, however, it might be better to stay close to the fence, then later turn right to follow a wall towards the summit of Meaul. Either way, the ground gets a bit rockier towards the top of the hill and there is a trig point at 695m as well as a cairn.

Only a vague path leads down from Meaul to the next gap. It's a slope punctuated by bits of rock, while the gap is fairly smooth, but bears small pools of water and rashes of stones in the short grass. Two vague paths leave the gap, but neither of them runs all the way to the summit of Carlin's Cairn. The ascent is usually at a fairly gentle gradient, starting on short grass which later becomes coarse in places. There are some stony patches with small outcrops of rock, but generally the surface of the broad crest of the hill is fairly smooth. A path reappears towards the summit, where there's more rock and finally an enormous cairn at 807m. This has been fashioned into a windbreak and from it you can enjoy extensive views over the more rugged parts of the Galloway Hills.

To start the descent, continue along the broad crest of the hill and aim for the great, grassy bulk of Corserine. The drop down to a gap leads across cobbles and gravelly patches. The gap itself is broad and grassy and you leave it by turning to the right. A steep slope leads down to Kirreoch Burn and you should walk roughly parallel to the burn down a very rugged moorland slope. There is plenty of tussocky grass, heather and bog to negotiate. A forestry plantation clothes the opposite bank of Kirreoch Burn, but once the edge of the forest takes a step back from the burn, you should cross over the burn. Follow the forest fence across the slope of the hill, then turn left to enter the forest along a short forest ride. Turn right along another ride and follow this down to the end of a forest road.

The forest road is quite mossy at its end and it swings off to the left as it runs downhill. On the right side of the road is a stout post and a few fire beaters, which stand at the top end of a forest ride. Follow this ride downhill to cross Kirreoch Burn again. Cross a broad rise beyond the burn, walking through tussocky grass and boggy bits, to reach another forest road. Turn right when you hit the road, then follow the road, which keeps fairly level and leads back to the junction where you parked your car near Gala Lane.

Carlin's Cairn

When Robert the Bruce was being hunted all over the Galloway Hills in 1307, he spent some time in hiding at Polmaddie Mill, where he was almost discovered by the soldiers who were pursuing him. In gratitude to the miller and his wife, he later called them to Loch Doon Castle and gave them land, money and the freehold of the mill. The miller's wife wanted to make some sort of gesture in return, and later persuaded her neighbours to assist with the construction of a huge cairn, Carlin's Cairn, which would be a landmark for miles around.

⁂ ⁂ ⁂

WALK 17: CARLIN'S CAIRN AND CORSERINE FROM POLMADDIE

There's a splendid walk around the head of Polmaddy Burn which takes walkers across Cairnsgarroch, Meaul, Carlin's Cairn and Corserine. The drawback is that a lengthy walk-in is required through Dundeugh Forest first - fully 6 miles (10km) both in and out! Unless you could take a car along the forest road by permission of the Forestry Commission, you'd have no option but to walk. You could base yourself at the Castlemaddy Scout Hut and thus shorten the distance by operating from that point, but the nearby Shiel of Castlemaddy Bothy was burnt down in recent years and may not be replaced in the future. Once you're clear of Dundeugh Forest, however, you can walk a superb skyline route around the head of the valley and savour extensive views across the Galloway Hills. Most of the higher parts of the walk are quite easy, but the hills are flanked by steep, rugged slopes which can be more difficult. If you didn't want to turn the walk round on Corserine, you could continue over the hill and drop down to the Backhill of Bush Bothy for the night instead.

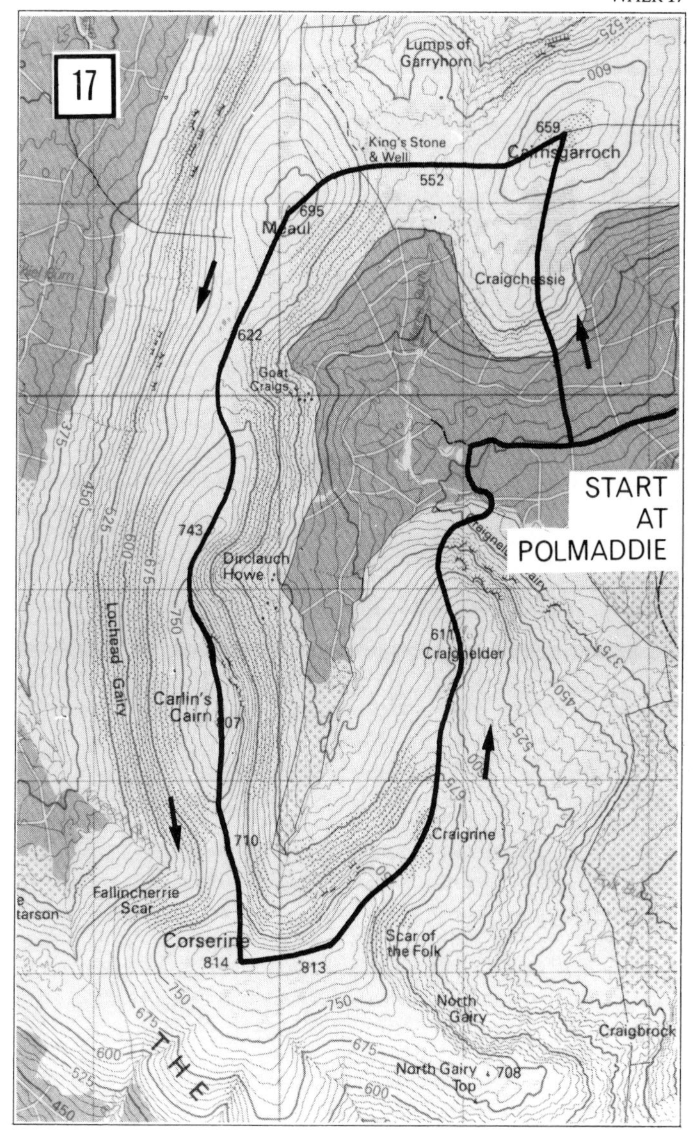
17
Lumps of Garryhorn
659
Cairnsgarroch
King's Stone & Well
552
695
Meaul
Craigchessie
622
Goat Craigs
START AT POLMADDIE
743
Dirclauch Howe
Lochead Gairy
611
Craignelder
Carlin's Cairn
807
Craigrine
710
Fallincherrie Scar
Corserine
814
813
Scar of the Folk
North Gairy
Craigbrock
North Gairy Top
708
THE

The Route

Distance: A long, moderate hill walk of 20 miles (32km).

Start: On the A713 at Polmaddie - 598880.

Parking: By the main road, close to the forest road.

The road serving Dundeugh Forest starts at Polmaddie on the A713 and initially runs close to Polmaddy Burn. After a gentle ascent away from the riverside, the road crosses Polmaddy Burn and rises gently to the Castlemaddy Scout Hut. Continuing ever further into the forest, the road climbs across the slopes of Gairy Craig and keeps well above the ruined Shiel of Castlemaddy Bothy. Be sure to keep left at a junction of forest roads before ascending gently across the slopes of Cairnsgarroch. Now is the time to start looking uphill along forest rides. You're looking for a ride which offers a clear view through to Craigchessie, a rugged shoulder of Cairnsgarroch.

Turn right off the forest road and walk up through the forest ride. At the edge of the forest, the boundary fence has collapsed so there's direct access to the open hillside. The steep slope directly ahead is clothed in grass, bilberry and boulders. There's a tree sprouting from a small crag ahead and you'll find it best to keep to the left of it. Despite the rugged start, the hillside becomes easier to negotiate as height is gained and eventually the land levels out in a broad, boggy area. Aim towards the summit of Cairnsgarroch in the distance, crossing a fence on the way and maybe passing a boulder which has been finished off with a cairn. The ground becomes rockier as the top of Cairnsgarroch is approached and there's a cairn at 659m. Views stretch from the flanks of the Rhinns of Kells to the massive bulk of Cairnsmore of Carsphairn.

A ruined wall crosses the top of Cairnsgarroch and this offers a guide all the way to the top of Meaul. Turn left to follow it away from the summit of Cairnsgarroch. As it runs down to a broad, grassy, boggy gap a fence accompanies it, the same fence which was crossed on the ascent. Just as you start climbing above the gap, look in the grass for a tumbled heap of stones and an old, broken stove, the remains of a shepherd's bothy. A little further uphill, you could detour off to the right to have a look at the King's Stone and Well. There are three rough stone chairs arranged around a rock slab where water seeps from the hillside. The fence following the wall later runs off to the left, but another fence runs in from the right higher up the slope. The wall continues towards the top of Meaul and the ground gets rockier near the top of the hill. There is a trig point at 695m, as well as a cairn.

Only a vague path leads down from Meaul to the next gap. It's a slope punctuated by bits of rock, while the gap is fairly smooth, but bears small pools of water and rashes of stones in the short grass. Two vague paths leave the gap, but neither of them runs all the way to the summit of Carlin's Cairn. The ascent is usually at a fairly gentle gradient, starting on short grass which later becomes coarse in places. There are some stony patches with small outcrops of rock, but generally the surface of the broad crest of the hill is fairly smooth. A path reappears towards the summit, where there's more rock and finally an enormous cairn at 807m. This has been fashioned into a windbreak and from it you can enjoy extensive views over the more rugged parts of the Galloway Hills.

To reach Corserine, continue along the broad crest of the hill and drop down to a gap. The way down crosses cobbles and gravelly patches before landing on a broad and grassy gap. The great, grassy bulk of Corserine rises above the gap, and a gradual pull up from the gap levels out on the broad, grassy and stony top of the hill. Corserine has a trig point at 814m, and a small, rather flat cairn. The broad top of the hill tends to obscure views into the valleys, but you'll see more on the descent from the summit. Stay near the steep, stony northern face of the hill to walk across to the next rise of Corserine at 813m. This bears a cairn. Now swing gradually north-eastwards for a descent on ground punctuated with small outcrops of rock. There is a vague vehicle track on this broad crest which can be traced downhill for a while.

Craigrine and Craignelder are two rocky bumps on the crest which are separated by a gentle, stony slope. Both humps have recently sprouted tall, slender masts bearing whirling windmills, but these have a temporary look about them and may well be either removed or replaced by more permanent structures. Be careful on the way down from Craignelder, as you need to avoid the ferociously rocky face of Craignelder Gairy. Keep well to the left when descending from the 611m summit cairn, picking the least rocky way down to Polmaddy Burn. You also need to be studying the arrangement of forest rides across the burn, which you've yet to negotiate to get back onto the forest road. Cross over Polmaddy Burn, then go round a corner on the forest to cross another tributary burn. Turn left along a forest ride which is almost completely closed by trees at one point, then pass a point where water splashes into a tiny pool. Continue along the forest ride, but turn right to follow another short ride which leads up to the forest road. Turn right to start walking along the road. You'll quickly pass the ride used to gain access to Cairnsgarroch earlier in the day, and all you need to do is to retrace your steps through the whole of Dundeugh Forest to return to your starting point - whether it was the Castlemaddy Scout Hut or the distant A713 at Polmaddie.

Polmaddie Mill

Robert the Bruce was being hotly pursued by soldiers when he came across Polmaddie Mill and sought refuge there. He let the miller's wife know of his identity, and she was willing to help him, but she explained that her husband was actually a supporter of Comyn, whom the Bruce had recently slain. However, it was the miller who hid him under some sacking when the soldiers came to search the mill. One story relates that a soldier actually cut through some dusty sacking shielding Robert the Bruce, almost choking the man. Despite near discovery at the mill, the Bruce lived to continue his struggle to retain the Scottish throne and fight for independence.

❊ ❊ ❊

WALK 18: CORSERINE FROM BACKHILL OF BUSH

Corserine is a broad, flat-topped, grassy hill at a junction of broad ridges. Most of the time, you'd have to park a long way from the hill and would expect a long day's walk over its slopes. However, you can also base yourself at the Backhill of Bush Bothy on the forested slopes of the hill and the walk to the summit from that point is really quite short. Forest roads allow an easy start and finish to the walk and the grassy slopes are easily walked with few difficulties. In misty conditions, however, the hill seems almost featureless and your navigation would need to be quite good. If you were to come off in the wrong direction you could find this easy and short circuit becoming long and tiring.

The Route

Distance: A moderate hill walk of 6½ miles (11km).

Start: At Backhill of Bush Bothy - 481843.

Parking: For overnight parking use the Craigencallie car park.

Leave the Backhill of Bush Bothy, turning right along the nearby forest road. This runs uphill very gently and you turn right along the next forest road too. Climbing a little more steeply, the second forest road is mossy and almost grass-grown in places. Follow it to its very end where a little burn is almost hidden in deep vegetation.

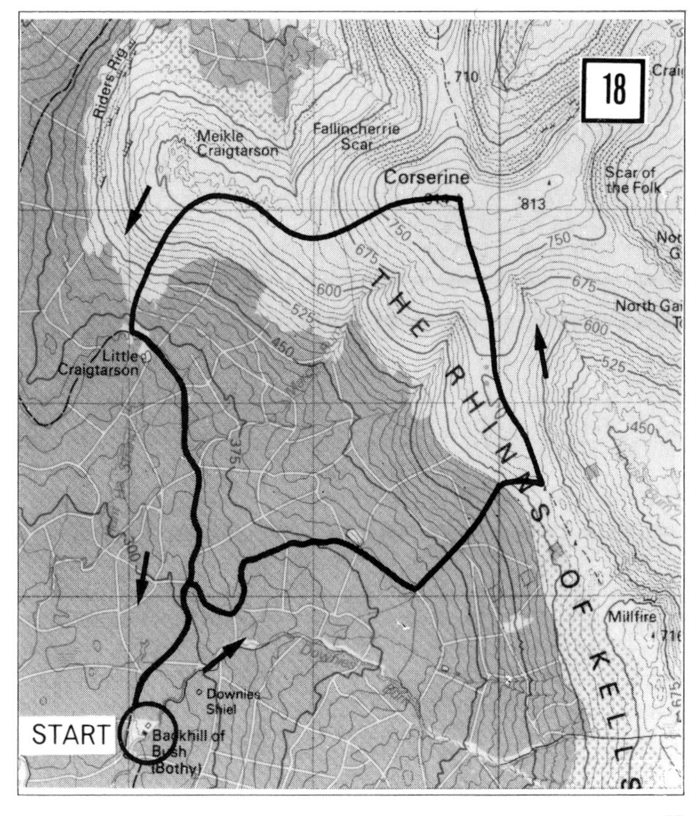

Turn left and follow the burn upstream. It runs along a forest ride which climbs more steeply uphill. Avoid any other rides to the left and right, so that the edge of the forest is reached fairly quickly. Bear a little to the right on reaching the open hillside and you'll reach a broad gap on the main crest of the Rhinns of Kells. Turn left and walk along the hummocky ridge, which bears a vague path in places. The path leads up the broad, grassy slopes of Corserine, but eventually vanishes. You'll have to navigate to the summit carefully in mist, looking for the trig point at 814m, which is surrounded by short grass and patches of stones. There is also a rather flat cairn on top. The broad top of the hill tends to obscure views into the valleys, but you'll see more on the descent from the summit. The rugged ranges of the Galloway Hills are displayed to the west, while the smooth outline of the bulky Cairnsmore of Carsphairn is off to the east.

Head roughly westwards from the trig point to start the descent. The slope gradually steepens, but later the gradient becomes gentler. However, the ground becomes more rugged underfoot on the hummocky crest of Meikle Craigtarson. Forge across this broad spur, passing small pools of water, then swing off to the left. A steep slope leads down on the forested slopes of the hill, but you should be looking carefully for a gap in the forest cover where only a few odd trees have been planted. Exploit this gap to reach a broad bend in a forest track, being careful of a sudden break in the slope at a small quarry. Once you hit the forest road, turn left and follow it gently downhill. It passes the mossy forest road which was used earlier in the day, then you'll later see the Backhill of Bush Bothy off to the left.

The Backhill of Bush Bothy

Backhill of Bush was formerly a shepherd's dwelling, in the days before forests were planted across the broad flanks of the Rhinns of Kells. Ruined sheepfolds can still be found in the gloom of the forests. At one time the nearest neighbours were beside Loch Doon or at Black Laggan. Despite occasional abuse, the bothy is well maintained and it could accommodate quite a few walkers. There are two rooms downstairs, one with a stove and one with a fireplace, plus a small room under the stairs. The stairs lead up to a long room under the roof. Logs are left in a pile by the forest road a short walk from the porch, and there are usually saws hung on the wall so that you can cut them into lengths. You would need to bring in an axe to chop the sawn logs for fuel. There is a nearby burn which goes by the name of Hunt Ha Strand, and in previous centuries Hunt Ha was a sort of shooting lodge where farmers and shepherds would gather to hunt foxes and deer. Despite the forbidding remoteness of these hills, there always seems to have been a few dwellings used at least for part of the year.

* * *

WALK 19: MILLDOWN FROM BACKHILL OF BUSH

Staying at the Backhill of Bush Bothy can save walkers having to endure lengthy walk-ins to complete some of the walks on the Rhinns of Kells. However, the accommodation is basic and all you really get is a roof over your head and the option of a log fire. The walk described below starts from the bothy and climbs onto the main crest of the Rhinns of Kells. After reaching the summit of Milldown the route comes down the forested slopes of the hill and ends with a sting in its tail. The rugged crest of Craigeazle is a strugglesome walk and a final forest ride is quite difficult to descend. However, if you leave Milldown with very little energy to spare, you could always return to the Backhill of Bush Bothy by way of a lengthy walk along forest roads. Alternatively, if you've bags of energy you might want to stay on the rugged crest and continue over the summits of Meikle and Little Millyea, Darrou and Craigwhannel.

The Route

Distance: An 8½ mile (14km) hill walk which starts easy and gets harder.

Start: At Backhill of Bush Bothy - 481843.

Parking: For overnight parking use the Craigencallie car park.

Leave the Backhill of Bush Bothy, turning right along the nearby forest road. This runs uphill very gently and you turn right along the next forest road too. Climbing a little more steeply, the second forest road is mossy and almost grass-grown in places. Follow it to its very end where a little burn is almost hidden in deep vegetation. Turn left and follow the burn upstream. It runs along a forest ride

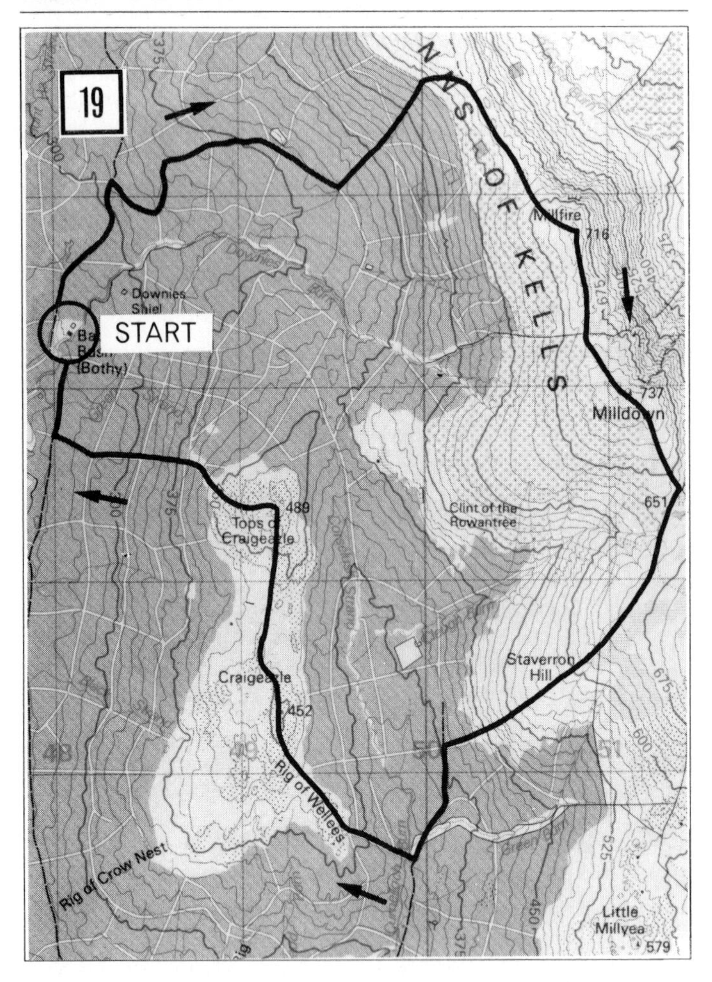

which climbs more steeply uphill. Avoid any other rides to left and right, so that the edge of the forest is reached fairly quickly. Bear a little to the right on reaching the open hillside and you'll reach a broad gap on the main crest of the Rhinns of Kells. Keep to the right and you'll pick up a path along the hummocky ridge. The path is narrow in places, but it's practically continuous as it climbs the rugged grassy and rocky slopes of Millfire. There are two cairns on the 716m summit. Walk further along the rugged crest of the hill to reach a junction of two walls. One of the walls has metal spikes sticking out of its top and this leads over the 737m summit of Milldown. From time to time along the crest you'll have splendid views down the rugged eastern flanks to Loch Dungeon.

Keep following the wall over Milldown to start the descent. A rugged slope leads down to a gap where you'll find a pool of water which is the largest of the Lochans of Auchniebut. The ground on the gap is usually boggy. Turn right and follow a fence away from the wall and pool. This crosses a broad moorland slope, then begins to run gently downhill. Leave the fence at a corner where a line of old posts comes in from the right. There is nothing to assist your navigation across the rugged, boggy, tussocky grass slopes of Staverron Hill, but it helps if you aim towards distant Loch Dee. The ground steepens and there is heather and outcropping rock. Look carefully along the forest edge to locate a ride which leads down to a forest road. Once you hit the road, turn left and enjoy a short, easy walk gently downhill. The road crosses Green Burn, then you should turn off to the right after a short while and cross Curneloch Burn when you see a gap in the forest. Once across the burn, a very vague path leads up a forest ride and emerges onto the Rig of Wellees. This is a tough moorland crest which features tussocky grass, heather, patches of bog and rock. It all adds up to a hard walk across Craigeazle to reach the Tops of Craigeazle at 489m. There's no path or natural line, so you choose a route which suits you best.

Head roughly westwards from the Tops of Craigeazle, then bear to the right along the top edge of the forest. You're looking for a gap in the trees which is used by deer and goats, which leads to a junction of forest rides. Take the ride which runs steeply downhill, avoiding all others to the left and right. It's heavy going at first, but the gradient and conditions underfoot get easier. Beware of areas where bog myrtle grows, as there are old lopped-off branches hidden in the grass which could trip you. Also watch out for a couple of nasty ditches which need to be crossed before you finally land on the forest road. After that difficult descent, it's simply a matter of turning right and walking back along the forest road to the Backhill of Bush Bothy.

Looking along the broad crest to Corserine from Millfire

Backhill of Bush

Life must have been hard for anyone living and working in the remote Backhill of Bush. A woman at Newton Stewart told me some of her great-aunt's experiences of life there. She had married a shepherd who worked there for a season and she had a babe in arms at the time. Finding herself afflicted with toothache, the woman had to walk over the Rhinns of Kells to visit the dentist at Dalry, leaving the baby with the shepherd. When the poor man was driven to distraction by the wailing infant, he set off over the Rhinns of Kells with the baby on his shoulder and met his wife coming home. She breast-fed the hungry babe on the open hillside and peace was restored. Such tales would at one time have been commonplace. The family later moved to a house by the Water of Minnoch, close to where Glentrool Village now stands. In later years, sheep rearing suffered a hard economic blow and those isolated dwellings were abandoned. In more recent times, much of the land was given over to forestry.

❊ ❊ ❊

WALK 20: TOPS OF CRAIGEAZLE FROM BACKHILL OF BUSH

If the cloud is hanging low over the Dungeon Hills and the Rhinns of Kells, or if sloppy snow makes it inadvisable to head for the highest hills, then you might be inclined to set your sights lower when looking for a walk from the Backhill of Bush Bothy. By using forest roads, it's possible to walk most of the way round the lower slopes of Craigeazle. A difficult walk leads over the Tops of Craigeazle and makes a circuit which ends back at the bothy. Although the crest of the hill is fairly low, it is also very rugged, but at least you'd be enjoying some sort of walk instead of festering all day at the bothy.

The Route

Distance:	A 7 mile (11km) walk which starts easy but gets harder.
Start:	At Backhill of Bush Bothy - 481843.
Parking:	For overnight parking use the Craigencallie car park.

Leave the Backhill of Bush Bothy, turning left along the nearby forest road. This has a couple of bends where it crosses Downies Burn, then it runs almost due south for some time. There are a couple of short rides leading off to the right, so that you can see the exceptionally rugged flanks of the Dungeon Hills - you might like to bear these access points in mind for future reference. The forest road swings round to the left at the Rig of Crow Nest and settles down to run south-eastwards. Immediately after crossing Curnelloch Burn there's another forest road turning off to the left. Follow this road uphill at a gentle gradient. As you climb, you'll sometimes be aware of running water off to the left in the trees. This is Curnelloch Burn again, but don't go down to its banks until you have a clear view of it at a point where there's a gap in the trees - just before the forest road crosses Green Burn.

Turn off to the left and cross Curnelloch Burn. A very vague path leads up a forest ride and emerges onto the Rig of Wellees. This is a tough moorland crest which features tussocky grass, heather, patches of bog and rock. It all adds up to a hard walk across Craigeazle to reach the Tops of Craigeazle at 489m. There's no path or natural line, so you choose a route which suits you best. Head roughly westwards from the Tops of Craigeazle, then bear to the

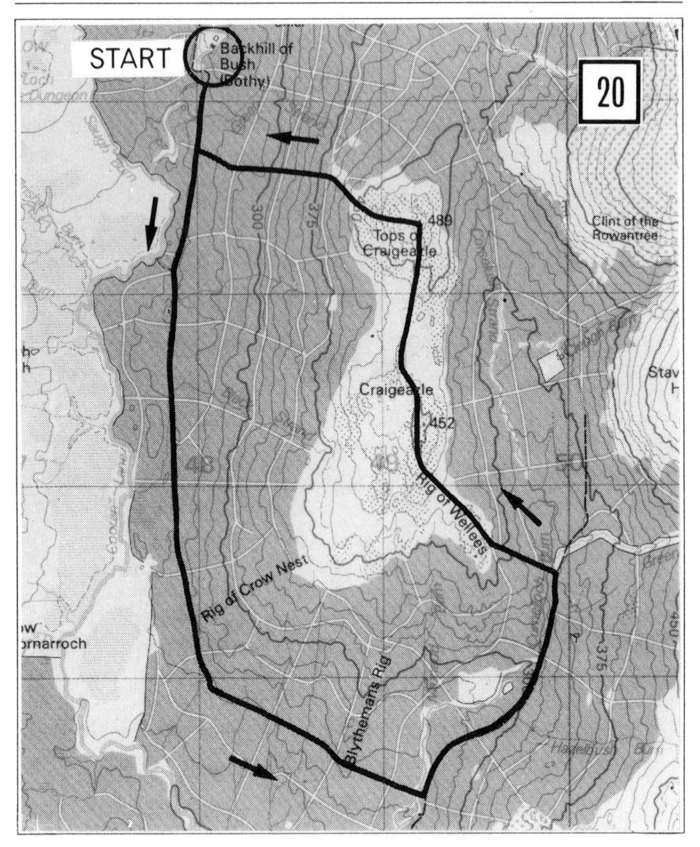

right along the top edge of the forest. You're looking for a gap in the trees which is used by deer and goats, which leads to a junction of forest rides. Take the ride which runs steeply downhill, avoiding all others to the left and right. It's heavy going at first, but the gradient and conditions underfoot get easier. Beware of areas where bog myrtle grows, as there are old lopped-off branches hidden in the grass which could trip you. Also watch out for a couple of nasty ditches which need to be crossed before you finally land on the forest road. After that difficult descent, it's simply a matter of turning right and walking back along the forest road to the Backhill of Bush Bothy.

* * *

WALK 21: DARROU, LITTLE MILLYEA & MEIKLE MILLYEA

The southern end of the Rhinns of Kells is very rough country underfoot, with boggy bits and bouldery bits as well as coarse vegetation to hinder your steps. A circular walk is offered below, leading over four rugged heights, each one being higher than the previous one. The walk turns around on Meikle Millyea, just when the ground is getting easier to cover, then a descent leads to a forest road for a long walk-out. There's no reason why you shouldn't extend the walk to Corserine, or even finish by the more distant shores of Loch Doon, rather than returning to the start at Craigencallie. The walk could also be attempted using the White Laggan Bothy or Backhill of Bush Bothy as bases.

The Route

Distance: A difficult hill walk of 9 miles (15km).

Start: At Craigencallie - 504781.

Parking: By the forest road gate at Craigencallie.

Leave by the little roadside car park at Craigencallie and go over the stile by the gate on the forest road. The road keeps low on the slopes of Cairnarroch at first, then you turn off to the right along another forest road to cross the River Dee. Turn right again at a large, triangular junction of forest roads, then head off to the left to enter a small, boulder-strewn quarry. The reason for entering the quarry is so that you can avoid tough vegetation on the lower slopes of Craigwhannel. By walking up to the top end of the quarry on a stony surface, progress uphill is given a little boost. There's a very steep, rugged strip of bracken, grass and heather which has been left unforested, and this allows access to the hummocky top of Craigwhannel. The summit area is composed of tussocky grass, heather and a few boulders. Head towards the next height, which is called Darrou, by passing a pool on a low, boggy gap nearby. The short climb is hard work, with deep heather, and finally leads to a

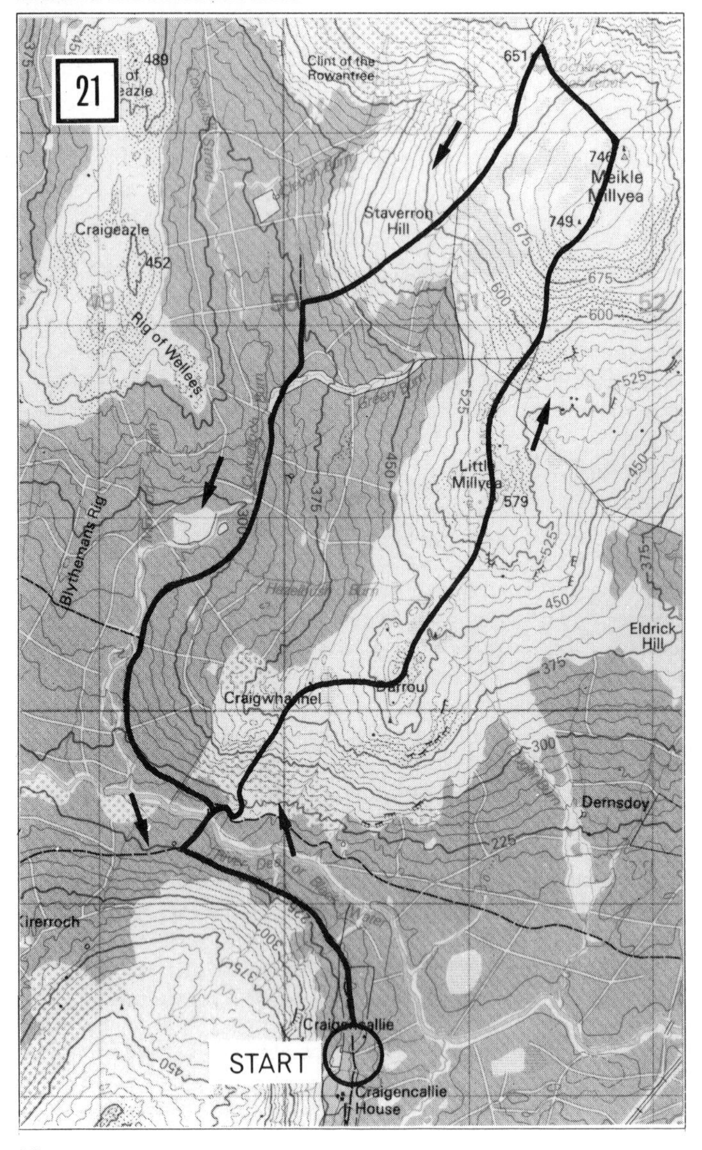
21
489
Clint of the
Rowantree
651
746
Meikle
Millyea
749
Staverron
Hill
Craigeazle
452
Rig of Wellees
Blythemans Rig
Little
Millyea
579
Eldrick
Hill
Craigwhannel
Darrou
Dernsdoy
Kirerroch
START
Craigencallie
Craigencallie
House

summit area with a scattering of boulders at under 500m.

The next hill in line along this difficult crest is Little Millyea. Again, there is the tough grass, heather and bog cover to negotiate, as well as low outcrops to avoid before the 579m summit is reached. There are some patches of bilberry which occur from time to time too. As you descend from Little Millyea, look ahead across a broad, rugged gap. There's a ruined wall to cross as you start climbing from the gap, then you should drift across bouldery ground to climb alongside another wall. The uphill pull is a mixture of rock, heather, grass and bilberry, but the wall finally leads onto a broad, grassy summit scattered throughout with patches of stones and with small outcrops of rock poking through. You can rest at the 749m summit cairn and admire the extensive views around the hills.

Walk further alongside the wall to cross the top of the hill, passing a trig point which you might notice on the other side of the wall at 746m. The wall runs down to a gap where you'll find a pool of water which is the largest of the Lochans of Auchniebut. The ground on the gap is usually boggy. Turn left and follow a fence away from the wall and pool. This crosses a broad moorland slope, then begins to run gently downhill. Leave the fence at a corner where a line of old posts comes in from the right. There is nothing to assist your navigation across the rugged, boggy, tussocky grass slopes of Staverron Hill, but it helps if you aim towards distant Loch Dee. The ground steepens and there is heather and outcropping rock. Look carefully along the forest edge to locate a ride which leads down to a forest road. Once you hit the road, turn left and enjoy the easy walk downhill. The forest road runs fairly close to Curnelloch Burn as it descends, then you should turn left at a junction of forest roads later. By following this forest road you'll reach the large, triangular junction of forest roads which was passed earlier in the day. Turn right at this point to cross the River Dee again, then turn left to follow the forest road back to the car park under the frowning face of Craigencallie.

Craigencallie

After being pursued across the Dungeon Hills in 1307 and surviving a couple of attempts of his life, Robert the Bruce reached Craigencallie alone to wait for his tiny army to reassemble. He sought shelter at Craigencallie where an old woman guessed his identity almost immediately. He asked her if she had any menfolk who might aid his pitifully small force, and she produced her three sons, by three different husbands - McKie, Murdoch and McLurg. They each demonstrated their skills with the bow and arrow. McKie picked off two ravens with one arrow as they passed the nearby cliffs. Murdoch took a single raven with his arrow, while McLurg shot close, but missed. The Bruce was suitably impressed and drafted all three into aiding his struggle against the advancing forces.

Knowing the countryside in some detail, the three men offered a plan of action as Robert the Bruce's army reassembled. Speaking in loud voices and blowing horns, the men gathered together herds of animals and kept them moving through the night. It sounded to the English camp as though a great army was gathering and their morale fell. Leaving the old woman in charge of herding the beasts, the Bruce's small force struck at the English camp before dawn. Imagining themselves caught in a pincer action, the English fled in confusion, unfortunately choosing to cross the boggy ground of Raploch Moss. As the day dawned, the Bruce's force picked off the mired army with a hail of arrows. It was another successful rout and another victory to Robert the Bruce, as always relying on a reading of the terrain and using it to his advantage. A stone commemorating the victory stands on the shore of Clatteringshaws Loch not far from the Deer Museum. It is thought that some tumbled stone walls across the road from Craigencallie House are the remains of the old woman's house and they carry the name of Bruce's Wa's. Craigencallie House is an outdoor pursuits centre where youngsters are introduced to a range of outdoor activities in the Galloway Hills.

Clatteringshaws Loch

The access road for Craigencallie stays close to the shores of Clatteringshaws Loch. The loch is actually a reservoir and is part of the Galloway Water Power Scheme which became operational in 1936. Most of the water running from the Galloway Hills is ultimately captured and used to turn the turbines in a series of hydro-electric power stations as far away as Tongland (which has visitor facilities). The reservoir covers most of the boggy ground of Raploch Moss, where Robert the Bruce defeated a large English force. Before the construction of the reservoir, local farmers cutting the peat for fuel were accustomed to turning up weaponry dating from the conflict of 1307.

* * *

Loch Macaterick and Loch Riecawr from Macaterick
Walking across the summit plateau of Corserine

Wild goats on the Galloway Hills near Black Loch
Looking to the Rhinns of Kells from Millfore

WALK 22: DARNAW AND COURT KNOWE FROM BLACK LOCH

The Queen's Road is a popular drive and one of the few main roads which comes really close to the Galloway Hills. Some of the attractions between New Galloway and Newton Stewart include the Bruce's Stone, Galloway Deer Museum, Red Deer Range, Wild Goat Park, Murray's Birthplace and Murray's Monument. There's also access to the shores of Clatteringshaws Loch and Craigencallie. A campsite is operated by the Forestry Commission nearby at Talnotry. The walk described below starts just off the Queen's Road at Black Loch, which lies at the back of the Red Deer Range and Wild Goat Park. The walk traces a section of the Old Edinburgh Road before making a very rough crossing of Darnaw. After descending close to Craigencallie, the return to Black Loch is via a forest road, which allows a quick and easy walk back to the car park. There may be time afterwards to study some of the attractions ranged along the Queen's Road.

The Route

Distance: A 10 mile (16km) walk which varies from hard to easy.

Start: At Black Loch - 500731.

Parking: There are two small car parks near Black Loch.

You can turn off the Queen's Road and follow the gravelly Craigdews Road to park near Black Loch. There are two small car parks, but try and use the first one if you can find space. The start of the walk is a little unclear, but have a look across the road from the car park. There is a gap in the trees which is deep in bracken, and if you forge a way through this gap you'll reach an overgrown trackway. This is the Old Edinburgh Road and if you turn right to follow it you'll cross Tonderghie Burn immediately and leave the forest nearby at a small waterfall. The old road is only two ruts wide in places, running through a vegetated hollow, but it is always clearly in view ahead. It runs uphill just below the boundary fence for the Red Deer Range, so look out for deer on the slopes of Brockloch Hill. The track passes a ruined observation hut near the fence, then runs into a small quarry. Walk straight along the forest road (not to the left) and you'll reach a parking space by some boggy ground near Lilie's Loch.

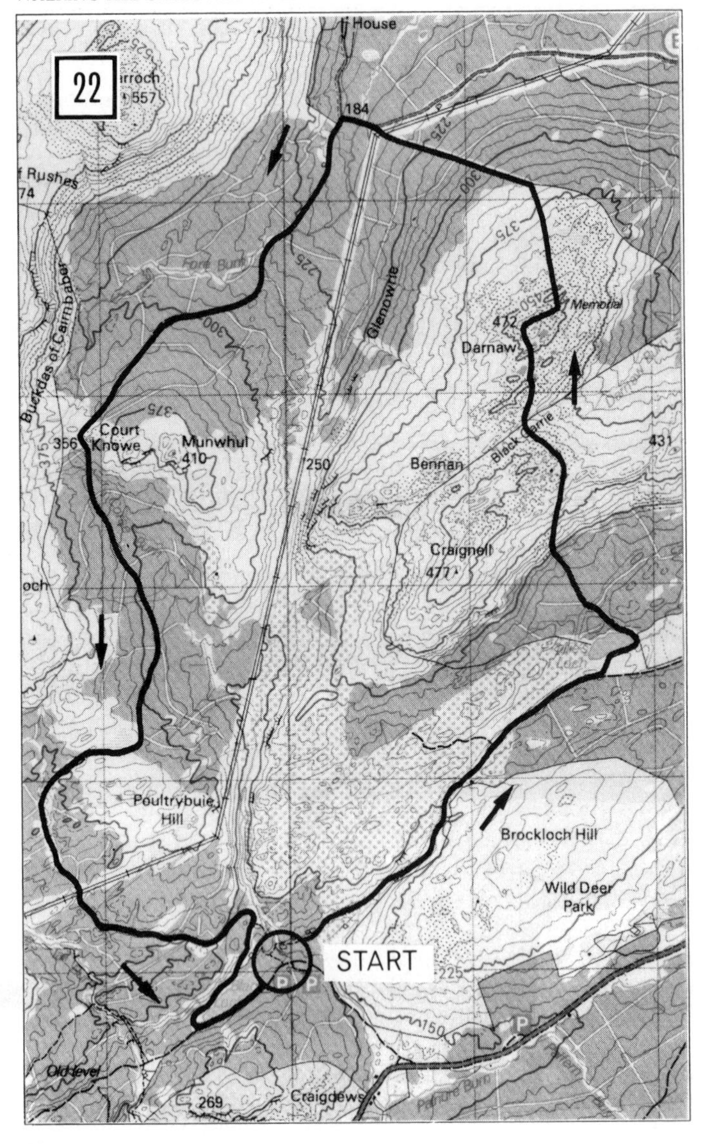
22
House
184
Rushes
Buckdas of Cairnbaber
Fore Burn
Glenowtie
Memorial
472
Darnaw
Court
Knowe
356
Munwhul
410
250
Bennan
Black Garrie
431
Craignell
477
Poultrybuie
Hill
Brockloch Hill
Wild Deer
Park
START
Old level
269
Craigdews
150
225
300
375
450

Follow a short path to the loch shore, then turn right and cross a burn flowing from the little loch. Enter the forest beyond by walking along a forest ride. This is boggy after an initial rise and bears tussocky grass in places. Avoid other rides which lead off to the right and left, and keep to the ride which runs up towards the rugged flank of Craignell. The ride is full of bracken as it runs towards the open hillside. Don't be discouraged at the steepness or rockiness of Craignell. Face the slope as you emerge from the forest and look carefully for a natural line of weakness rising diagonally to the right. You'll find that you can pick a way up and across the steep and rugged slope by following that line, without any need to grapple with rocks or plant your feet in precarious stances. After the steep climb, which is really quite short, you'll emerge on the hummocky crest of the hill and should be able to see Darnaw ahead. Pick any route which looks reasonable to reach Darnaw's summit. There is no path across the hummocky ground, which is a jumble of rocky outcrops, pools of water, boggy patches and heather. You'll cross a ruined fence on a rugged gap before climbing to the cairn on the 472m summit of Darnaw.

Head roughly north-east from the top of Darnaw, dropping a short way down the hillside towards Clatteringshaws Loch. There's a memorial cairn on the shoulder of the hill which you can inspect, then you head roughly north-west down the rugged grass and heather slopes to hit a ruined wall which leads down along a forest ride. Follow the wall down the ride, crossing heather, tussocky grass and bog myrtle on the way. At the bottom of the ride you pass beneath an electricity-pylon line before landing on a narrow tarmac road. Turn left to walk along the road, crossing a small burn on the way. Turn left at a corner to climb a stile by a gate, then follow a broad, firm, forest road. The road offers easy walking from this point onwards, climbing gradually at first alongside Fore Burn, leaving the forest briefly at Court Knowe at 356m. There's a descent for a while, then another gradual climb as the road crosses a broad gap near Poultrybuie Hill. There are generally good views all the way along the forest road as the trees aren't planted so as to totally obscure the surrounding hills. The final descent takes the road under the electricity-pylon line again. The road runs almost down to Tonderghie Burn, then all the way round the shore of Black Loch to end back at the two small car parks where you started.

The Red Deer Range

The walk skirts the fence of the Red Deer Range on Brockloch Hill. Although deer wander apparently at will and without hindrance throughout the hills and forests of the area, there are certain controls on their numbers. Red deer have always lived in the Galloway Hills, but with deforestation they became much less in number, as well as somewhat smaller. With the depopulation and reafforestation of the hills, they have again increased in number and size. They have no natural enemies, so they have to be culled, though this is usually a low-key process. There is no deer stalking as there is on some of the large estates elsewhere in Scotland, and hence there's no restrictions on access for walkers either. The Red Deer Range has been established to allow visitors a close-up view of these magnificent animals and further information can be obtained from the Galloway Deer Museum by the shores of Clatteringshaws Loch. Teas and snacks are also offered at the museum.

The Wild Goat Park

The so-called "wild" goats of the Galloway Hills probably have a very mixed ancestry. They are thought to have descended from Irish stock and may be feral rather than truly wild. However, their magnificent horns and shaggy coats certainly give them a wild appearance. They have made a home for themselves in the hills and large herds can be found grazing on the highest summits in the summer. The Wild Goat Park has been established to allow visitors a close-up view of these animals. You'll find them much more approachable than the deer next door.

Alexander Murray

Close to the Red Deer Range and the Wild Goat Park is an invitation for people to park their cars and visit Murray's Birthplace at Dunkitterick Cottage, or climb to Murray's Monument on a nearby hill. Alexander Murray was born in the low, stone cottage in 1775 into a shepherding family. At an early age he showed a great love for reading and writing, and was soon devouring every scrap of print which came his way. What little schooling he obtained was interrupted by ill health, but by the age of 13 he had mastered foreign languages and found them to be a fascinating study. Through a friendship with a part-time smuggler called McHugh, word

Looking along the Fore Burn near Craigencallie

reached academics in Edinburgh about the young Murray's abilities and he was soon enrolled as a student in the university. He died in 1813 at the age of 37 and many stories are told of his life and ability in the area. Murray's Monument was raised in his honour in 1834, while in 1975 - the bicentenary of Murray's birth - the walls of Dunkitterick Cottage were partially raised and consolidated against further decay.

Darnaw and the Dragon Fly

The memorial on Darnaw overlooking Clatteringshaws Loch was placed there to the memory of four people who were killed in an aircraft crash. The Daily Express aircraft Dragon Fly crashed on 2nd February 1937. There have been many other aircraft crashes in the Galloway Hills which are identified only by remaining fragments of wreckage scattered across the hillsides.

* * *

WALK 23: CAIRNARROCH AND MILLFORE FROM CRAIGENCALLIE

Millfore is a very aloof hill, with a deep gap separating it from its neighbours in the Minnigaff Hills. It can be climbed from the road at Craigencallie, or from the White Laggan Bothy, if you're using that as a base. An approach could also be made from Auchinleck and Drigmorn to the south. A good circuit can be enjoyed by climbing Millfore from Craigencallie, then descending by way of the White Laggan Bothy. A short stretch of the long-distance Southern Upland Way can be followed on the way back to Craigencallie. Parts of the walk are quite rugged, but in fine weather there's a tremendous all-round view from the summit. In foul weather at least there's an opportunity to seek shelter at the White Laggan Bothy - a handy base for explorations of the Minnigaff and Dungeon Hills.

The Route

Distance: A difficult hill walk of 9 miles (15km).

Start: At Craigencallie - 504781.

Parking: By the forest road gate at Craigencallie.

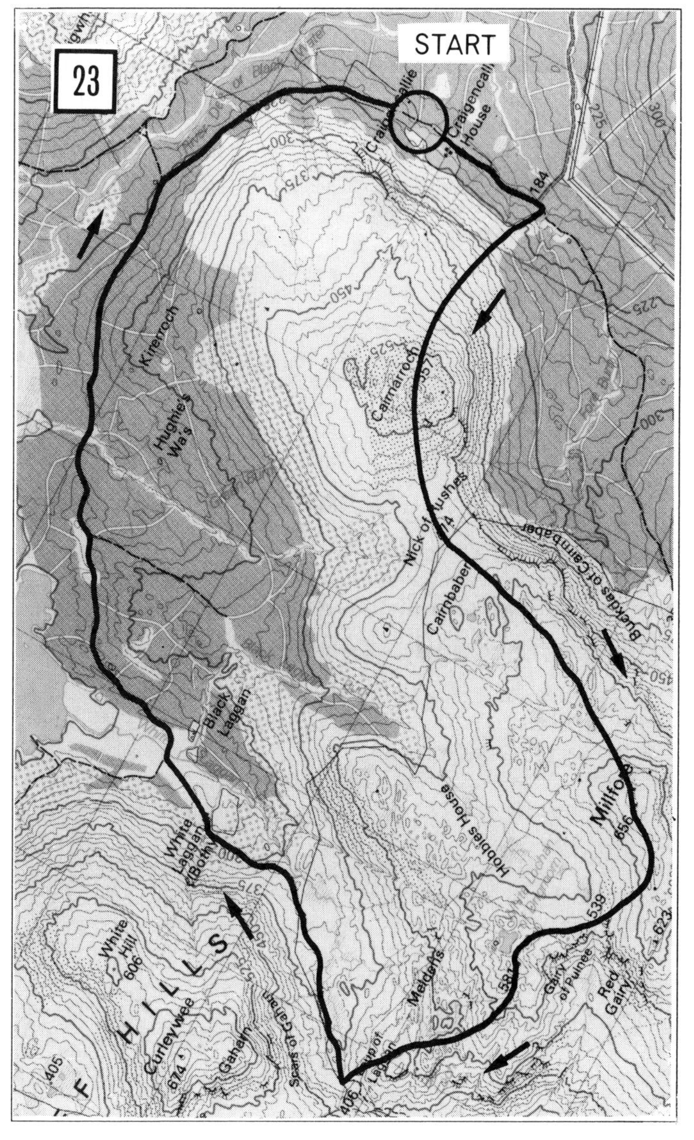
23
START
Craigencallie
Craigencallie House
184
Kirerroch
Hughie's Wa's
Cairnarroch
557
Nick of Rushes
Cairnbaber
Buckdas of Cairnbaber
Black Laggan
White Laggan (Bothy)
Hobbies House
Millfore
656
539
Gairy of Pulnee
Red Gairy
623
581
Meikle
White Hill
606
HILLS
Curleywee
674
Gaharn
Scars of Gaharn
405
406
300
375
450
525
225

Park at Craigencallie, then walk back along the road, passing the access road for Craigencallie House, to reach a sudden bend to the left. Go straight onwards at this bend, crossing a stile by a gate on a forest road. Almost immediately, turn to the right to leave the forest road and walk up a rugged slope which lies between two stands of forestry. There's some bracken to forge through at first, then higher slopes are clothed in tussocky grass and heather. There are also patches of bilberry before rocks start showing through the vegetation. Use heathery strips to zig-zag between shelves of rock as you climb ever upwards towards the summit of Cairnarroch. The gradient eases, but the ground is predominantly rocky. Aim for the summit cairn on Cairnarroch at 557m.

Head off the hill in a south-westerly direction, going down a rugged slope to reach a broad gap called the Nick of Rushes. A faint path leads uphill from the gap and you have to cross a fence. A broad, hummocky, grassy crest is followed uphill, so that you stay well away from the rocky slope called the Buckdas of Cairnbaber. You'll find yourself crossing a line of old fenceposts before the final pull up to the top of Millfore. There's a trig point on the 656m summit, as well as a couple of nearby cairns. There are excellent views around the Galloway Hills which include the Range of the Awful Hand, Dungeon Hills, Rhinns of Kells and Cairnsmore of Fleet.

Start the descent by following the summit crest of Millfore, then branch off to the right before reaching a subsidiary cairned summit. A steep, rugged slope leads down to a hummocky gap where a faint path can be picked up. This leads over a rise to the White Lochan of Drigmorn. There's a cairn on a hump beyond the lochan at 581m, then you need to take care descending the rest of the rugged ridge towards the Loup of Laggan. The slopes leading down to the gap are very rugged, with some hidden crags on the way. It's best to keep somewhat to the right of the ridge running down to the gap. You should notice a line of old fenceposts before reaching the gap. - the same line as the line which was seen on the ascent of Millfore. Turn right and follow an old road downhill from the Loup of Laggan to the White Laggan Bothy. This road is boggy in places, but always clearly in view ahead. There's a stile by a gate which you cross in a broad, boggy valley beneath Curleywee, then a descent towards the

The White Laggan Bothy beneath Curleywee

White Laggan Bothy. The bothy is in an area planted with young trees and shelter is available if required. To complete the walk, walk past the bothy and continue down a boggy path to reach a broad forest road near the ruins of Black Laggan. Turn right to follow the road, which is part of the Southern Upland Way. The road crosses forested slopes above Loch Dee, then later the Southern Upland Way turns off to the left. Make sure that you keep to the right, following the forest road around the lower slopes of Cairnarroch. The road leads back to the car park under the frowning face of Craigencallie.

A Wee Bit Hassock o' Land

When Robert the Bruce had succeeded in his immense struggle to retain the Scottish throne and independence for the country, he remembered to reward all those who had assisted him in his campaign. The old widow who lived at Craigencallie asked the Bruce for the "wee bit hassock o' land atween Palnure and Penkiln". Palnure Burn and Penkiln Burn are two rivers flowing from the Minnigaff Hills which eventually reach the broad curves of the Cree. While you're walking over the top of Millfore, you can look southwards across the rugged tract of land enclosed by the two rivers.

⁂ ⁂ ⁂

WALK 24: MILLFORE FROM AUCHINLECK

There's a deep gap at the Loup of Laggan which separates Millfore from its neighbours in the Minnigaff Hills. Millfore can be climbed from Craigencallie, where cars can be parked, or by anyone using the White Laggan Bothy as a base for exploring the Minnigaff Hills. However, the ascent described below is from Auchinleck and Drigmorn. A sort of horseshoe walk can be created by climbing Millfore, then crossing the Loup of Laggan and returning along the rugged crest of Bennan Hill. There's also the possibility of extending the walk by including an ascent of Curleywee. Views from both Millfore and Curleywee are very good. Auchinleck is off the edge of the map, but you're only missing the forest track which leads to Drigmorn from Auchinleck. To approach the start of the walk at Auchinleck you follow a minor road from Newton Stewart and Minnigaff which is called Cumloden Road. A sign along this road indicates Auchinleck and you can park before reaching the building.

The Route

Distance: A difficult hill walk of 11 miles (18km).

Start: At a bridge before Auchinleck - 447705.

Parking: Small parking space by the bridge.

There's a parking space by a bridge over Penkiln Burn, a short way before Auchinleck. Continue on foot along the road to pass the splendid house at Auchinleck. A rougher road continues beyond the house to enter a forest. Walk along the forest road, which runs roughly parallel to Pulbae Burn. You can either ford the burn to reach the old farmstead at Drigmorn, or go a little way upstream and cross an old bridge made of railway sleepers. There are a couple of large enclosures above Drigmorn which you pass through using gates to reach the open hillside beyond. Walk roughly northwards across boggy ground, aiming for the top of Drigmorn Hill directly ahead. The grassy hillside becomes firmer underfoot, but steepens as you progress upwards. There are odd cairns which have been raised on prominent humps and ridges, but they have no real significance as aids to navigation. Drigmorn Hill is only a distant shoulder of Millfore, but it is distinguished by the sudden appearance of a lochan on its crest. Walk roughly north-eastwards from the

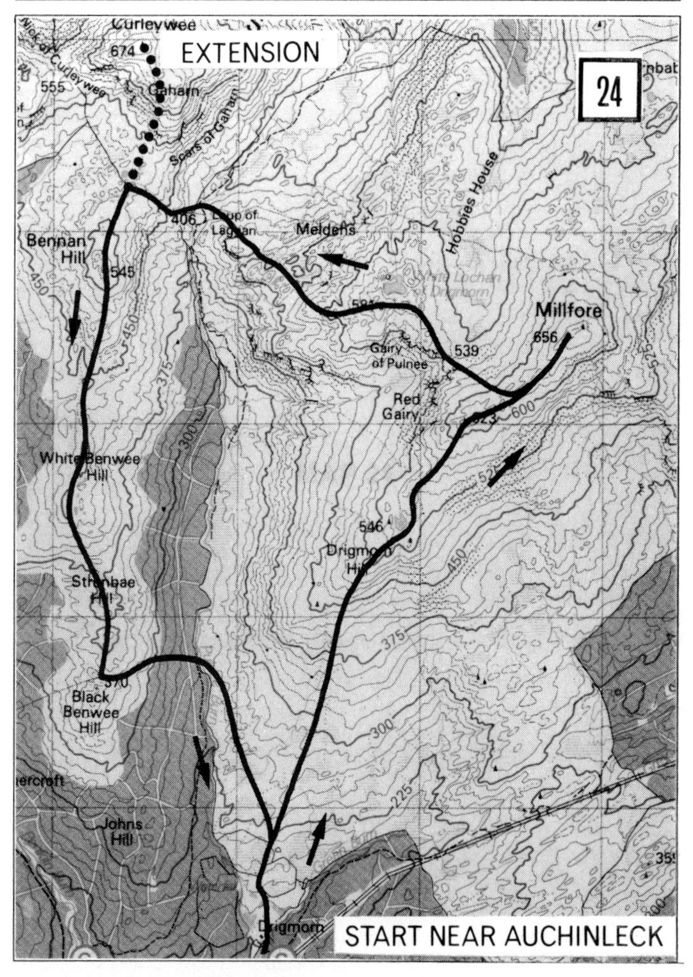

lochan, climbing to the 623m summit of Millfore. Now continue along the hummocky crest of the hill to reach the higher summit at 656m. Both of Millfore's summits bear cairns, but the higher one also has a trig point.

Start the descent by retracing your steps along the summit crest;

then branch off to the right before reaching the lower summit. A steep, rugged slope leads down to a hummocky gap where a faint path can be picked up. This leads over a rise to the White Lochan of Drigmorn. There's a cairn on a hump beyond the lochan at 581m, then you need to take care descending the rest of the rugged ridge towards the Loup of Laggan. The slopes leading down to the gap are very rugged, with some hidden crags on the way. It's best to keep somewhat to the right of the ridge running down to the gap, then you'll land on an old road which crosses the gap. A fence leads uphill from the gap and rises up a rugged slope to reach a broad, boggy, hummocky gap. You have the option of climbing Curleywee as an "extra" from there.

Turn left on the broad gap to follow the rugged crest to Bennan Hill's summit at 545m. Head southwards towards White Benwee Hill, picking a way across heather, bilberry and boggy areas. Head downhill again to cross the hump of Stronbae Hill to reach an old wall on a rocky, boggy gap before Black Benwee Hill. Turn left and follow the wall down a rugged slope The wall runs down a forest ride to reach Pulnee Burn, which you cross to reach the boggy ground on the opposite bank. Turn right to start following the burn downstream. Although you could follow the burn all the way to Drigmorn, it's probably better if you drift away from it up a boggy slope to the left. You'll reach the large enclosures you passed through earlier in the day and you simply go back through the gates to reach Drigmorn. All that remains is to cross Pulbae Burn, turn right and follow the forest road back past Auchinleck to return to the parking space by the bridge over Penkiln Burn.

Drigmorn

Alexander Murray spent some time living at Drigmorn, where his father moved at the advanced age of 82. Despite suffering ill health, the young Murray was able to attend school on and off through 1789, and in the same year he wandered around the hill farms teaching the children of three families who lived some distance apart. Another move took the Murrays to Barncaughlaw, closer to Minnigaff, where Alexander's education was greatly facilitated and he was able to study Latin, Greek and Hebrew. Amazingly, it's reckoned that he obtained only around a total of 60 hours of formal education. He had a friendship with the poet Robert Burns, but it was a part-time smuggler called McHugh who finally brought word of the young Murray's accomplishments to the notice of academics in Edinburgh. After studying at the university, Murray eventually became Professor of Oriental Languages and is fondly remembered in the area.

WALK 25: LAMACHAN HILL FROM AUCHINLECK

The valley of Penkiln Burn is heavily forested, but the open hills rise above the trees all round and a natural horseshoe walk suggests itself. The only problem is getting out onto the hills and getting back through the forests to end the walk. This walk makes use of handy forest rides and clear-felled areas which are easily accessible from the one forest road running through the valley. The walk starts off the edge of the map, but it's a simple walk-in along a forest road. Larg Hill, Lamachan Hill and Curleywee are the main heights on this round, with Garlick Hill, Bennan Hill and Benwee Hill being of lesser height, but more difficult underfoot. It's a good introduction to walking in the Minnigaff Hills, and views from the summits extend across the rest of the Galloway Hills. To approach the start of the walk at Auchinleck you follow a minor road from Newton Stewart and Minnigaff which is called Cumloden Road. A sign along this road indicates Auchinleck and you can park before reaching the building.

The Route

Distance:	A difficult hill walk of 12 miles (19km).
Start:	At a bridge before Auchinleck - 447705.
Parking:	Small parking space by the bridge.

There's a parking space by a bridge over Penkiln Burn, a short way before Auchinleck. A forest road branches off from the tarmac road at the bridge, and this is signposted as the Lamachan Road. Walk along the forest road, bearing to the right until the road is running roughly parallel to Penkiln Burn. The road climbs alongside the burn, then you need to turn off to the left when you reach a large, clear-felled and replanted area. Walk on a line roughly in-between the new plantation and the more mature forest, but note that this slope is covered in long grass, bracken, old lopped-off branches and boggy patches. There's also a little runnel of water which will lead you along a forest ride where you can gain easy access to the top edge of a forest. Continue uphill on a rugged moorland slope clothed in grass, heather, bilberry and broken rock. Turn right to follow a wall up onto Garlick Hill. You could make a short detour to include the summit trig point at 445m.

The wall runs down a short way from Garlick Hill and leads through a gap between two forestry plantations. By following a wall and fence to the right, you'll be led across a grassy, heathery moor close to the forest on Sheuchanower. The wall crosses the Nick of Sheuchan and climbs up onto Sheuchan Craig. Leaving the forest behind, the wall climbs up a broad, steep ridge and finally reaches the top of Larg Hill. There's a junction of walls on the lower part of the ridge and another junction of walls close to the tiny summit cairn at 676m. The top of the hill is broad and bears short grass and a peppering of stones. The view takes in the great bulk of Cairnsmore of Fleet to the south-east, and the rugged Range of the Awful Hand to the north. Better views of the Galloway Hills are obtained later on the round - from the summits of Lamachan Hill and Curleywee.

The walk to Lamachan Hill is simple. Just turn right on reaching the top of Larg Hill and follow the wall down to the Nick of the Brushy. The wall turns off to the left at the gap, but you continue straight on across the gap and pick up a line of old metal fenceposts. These lead up the broad, grassy slopes of Lamachan Hill. There are odd large boulders dotted around the slope, but the ascent is fairly gentle with no problems. There's an old wall running across the broad top of the hill which joins the line of old fenceposts at the 717m summit. Follow the fenceposts across the top of the hill and down to a subsidiary hump called Bennanbrack at 687m. The ground is rockier and the fenceposts suddenly head off to the right to go down a rugged ridge. Follow the fenceposts faithfully downhill, keeping to the right of a hump which is later observed to have a steep, rocky face. Continue down to a hummocky gap, then go down further to a lower gap called the Nick of Curleywee. Cross a fence and ruined wall on this gap, then make a direct ascent of Curleywee. There's a grassy strip which allows for a short, steep climb to the top of the hill, and there's a faint path you can use. A cairn marks the 674m

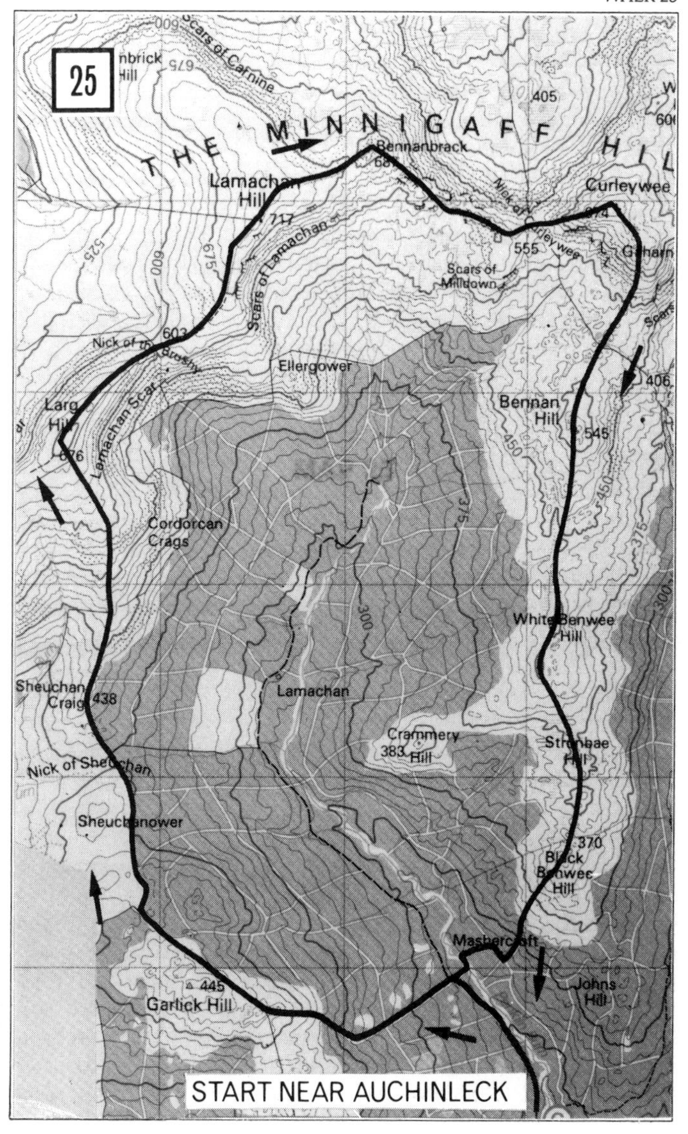
25
THE MINNIGAFF HILLS
Lamachan Hill
717
Bennanbrack
Curleywee
Nick of Curleywee
555
Scars of Lamachan
Scars of Milldown
Scars of Carnine
405
603
Nick of the Brushy
Ellergower
Larg Hill
676
Lamachan Scar
Bennan Hill
545
406
Cordorcan Crags
White Benwee Hill
Sheuchan Craig
438
Lamachan
Crammery Hill
383
Strohbae Hill
Nick of Sheuchan
Sheuchanower
370
Black Benwee Hill
Mashercroft
Johns Hill
445
Garlick Hill
START NEAR AUCHINLECK

summit and superb views stretch around the surrounding hills.

To leave Curleywee, wander along the broad crest of the hill to Gaharn, then bear right and walk down a steep, rugged slope of grass, heather and rock. There's a broad, boggy, hummocky gap to cross on the way to Bennan Hill, with a ruined wall and fence to cross first. Follow the rugged crest to Bennan Hill's summit at 545m. Head southwards towards White Benwee Hill, picking a way across heather, bilberry and boggy areas. Head downhill again to cross the hump of Stronbae Hill and cross an old wall on a rocky, boggy gap before Black Benwee Hill. When you reach the small cairn on top of Black Benwee Hill, bear to the right and descend. In clear weather you should aim for the left side of the prominent clear-felled patch on Garlick Hill - which was crossed earlier in the day's walk. A small hump above the top edge of the forest hides a forest ride. Follow the ride downhill, forging through the bracken which grows along it, then turn right along another ride. This is rather muddy in places, as is the next ride on the left which runs down to Penkiln Burn. Walk downstream a short way and cross over to the other side. A short walk uphill leads back onto the forest road. Simply turn left and retrace your early steps back along the forest road to return to the parking space by the bridge over Penkiln Burn.

❊ ❊ ❊

WALK 26: LARG HILL FROM CALDONS CAMPSITE

Larg Hill is a broad, grassy whaleback ridge with quite steep flanks. The actual ridge walk offers an easy and pleasant stroll, but the approach routes can be rather long and sometimes difficult. The hill seems aloof and distant in many views around Newton Stewart and Glen Trool. Forestry plantations close in on all sides, so that ascents and descents include time spent in the coniferous gloom. The circuit offered from Caldons Campsite makes use of a lengthy forest road which approaches the hill quickly and easily, though it seems never-ending. The grassy ridge walk is followed by a descent towards Craignaw, then the merry waters of Caldons Burn lead back down to the campsite. You can usually pick up basic food and drink at the campsite shop, depending on the opening times and seasons.

The rugged Curleywee as seen from Larg Hill

The Route

Distance:	A moderate hill walk of 10 miles (16km).
Start:	Near Caldons Campsite - 397791.
Parking:	Small parking spaces off the campsite access road.

Park near the bridge over the Water of Trool on the access road to Caldons Campsite. Head for the children's play area which is found to the right of the road before the campsite shop. Also on the right is a gate giving access to a forest road. Follow the forest road uphill through mixed woodland at first. Avoid a left turn where another forest road goes around Jenny's Hill, then avoid a right turn where a forest road heads off near a replanted area. After views over the replanted area, the forest road heads into more mature stands of forestry. Avoid yet another right turn, but be sure to take the next right turn along a broad forest road. This road is near level for a while, then it begins to climb gently. Look out on the left side for a stout stone wall which runs along a forest ride. Turn left to leave the forest road and follow the wall through the forest ride. There's tussocky grass and a small burn to cross, then the ascent features

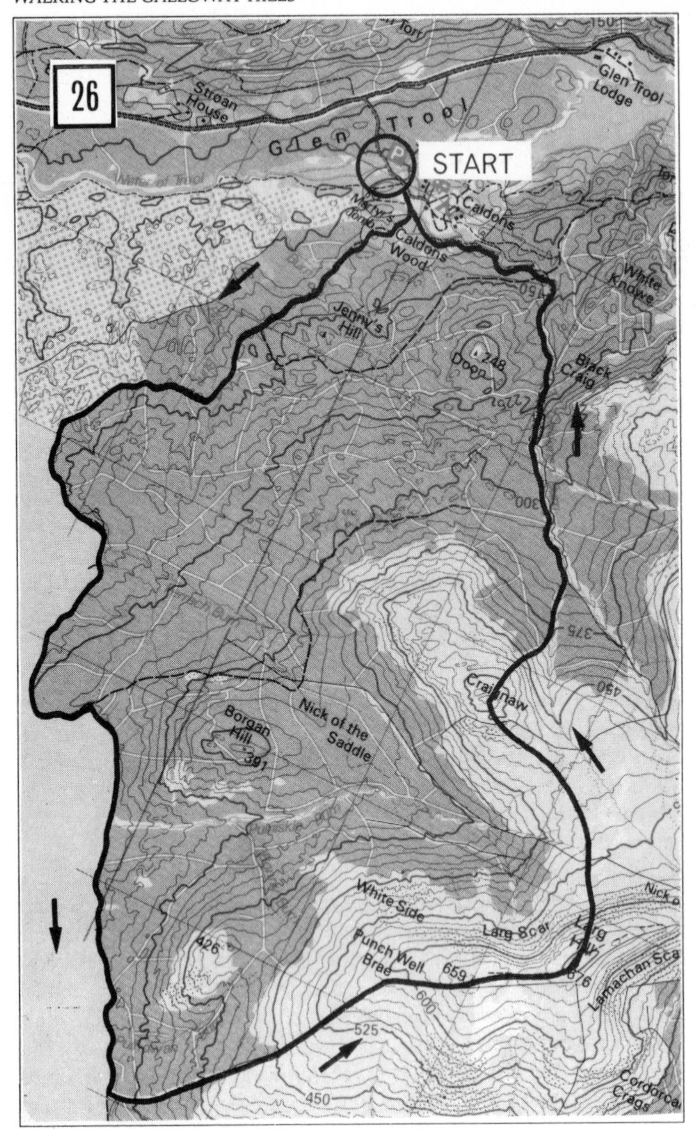
26
START
Glen Trool
Stroan House
Glen Trool Lodge
Caldons
Martyr's Tomb
Caldons Wood
White Knowe
Jenny's Hill
Doon
748
Black Craig
150
300
375
450
Craignaw
Borgan Hill
391
Nick of the Saddle
White Side
Larg Scar
Larg Hill
Punch Well Brae
659
676
Lamachan Sca
600
525
450
426
Cordorca
Crags
Nick o

patches of heather and bracken, but conditions underfoot get easier as height is gained. There's a fence to cross as the wall rises above the forest, then it's simply a case of following the wall up grassy slopes onto the top of Larg Hill. The hill has two summits, one at 659m and a further one at 676m. Both are marked by small summit cairns and there are stones peppered around the broad, grassy tops.

From the 676m summit, you should head towards the steep northerly face of the hill and pick a way down the slopes of broken rock and scree. Parsley fern finds a roothold on this type of surface, then there's a broad moorland gap to cross on the way to Craignaw. Heather and bilberry are crossed on the gap before the grassy, rocky slopes of Craignaw are reached. Cross a fence on the final pull up to the summit cairn.

Descend in a north-easterly direction, aiming to follow the edge of a forest down a steep, grassy slope. This leads down to a burn which you can follow downstream. The trees of the forest are planted rather close to the water, so you might find it best to walk first on one bank and then on the other. Before long, however, you should be on the western bank of Caldons Burn and stay on that side to finish the walk. The path is muddy in places, then you need to be careful above a steep-sided rocky gorge, which is full of waterfalls you'll hardly catch a glimpse of. The forest trees change to deciduous cover, which tells you that Caldons Campsite is nearby. There are some places where brambles are tangled across the path, but you'll soon emerge back at the children's play area at the campsite. A left turn along the campsite access road leads back to the car parks by the bridge. You could also follow a path to have a look at the Martyr's Tomb, signposted off to the left.

Caldons Campsite

Caldons Campsite is open to tents and caravans and offers a handy base for the exploration of the Galloway Hills. It is run by the Forestry Commission and has basic facilities including toilets, showers, telephone and small shop. It is on the long-distance Southern Upland Way, so is popular with walkers following that route, and there is very little accommodation on the route beyond that point until distant Dalry. The campsite is also at the junction of a number of waymarked trails - the Yellow Trail from Stroan Bridge and the Loch Trool Forest Trail which are also covered in this guide.

Although the campsite is quiet and in a pleasant setting, campers are at the mercy of midges on fine summer days and should come fully prepared to deal with them. The campsite shop sells repellents!

* * *

WALK 27: LAMACHAN HILL AND MULLDONOCH

Lamachan Hill is the tallest and broadest of the Minnigaff Hills and its central position in that group makes it a fine viewpoint, despite its rather broad shoulders. It's also a fairly smooth hill, which makes walking across it delightfully easy. Most of the approaches are quite rugged, while neighbouring Mulldonoch is rugged from head to toe. Mulldonoch is an isolated heap of rock, bog and heather. Its most northerly prow is White Bennan and you're being warned well in advance that the descent from the hills in that direction is very steep and difficult. It should not be attempted if there is snow, ice or frost on the ground. It was from those precipitous slopes that Robert the Bruce and his army ambushed a large English force, trundling boulders onto the soldiers and successfully routing the army. There are superb views across Glen Trool at the end of this walk, but if you think you could be struggling on the steep slopes, then consider taking the safer descent from the Nick of Lochans. Either way, the walk ends with a stretch of the long-distance Southern Upland Way in Glen Trool.

The Route

Distance: A difficult hill walk of 8½ miles (14km).

Start: Near Caldons Campsite - 397791.

Parking: Small parking spaces off the campsite access road.

Park near the bridge over the Water of Trool on the access road to Caldons Campsite. Head for the children's play area which is found to the right of the road before the campsite shop. Look carefully at the back of the play area for the start of a riverside path following Caldons Burn upstream. The path runs through woodlands and although there are brambles tangled across the path in places, the way becomes clearer later. Keep fairly close to Caldons Burn and note how the trees change from deciduous to coniferous cover. The

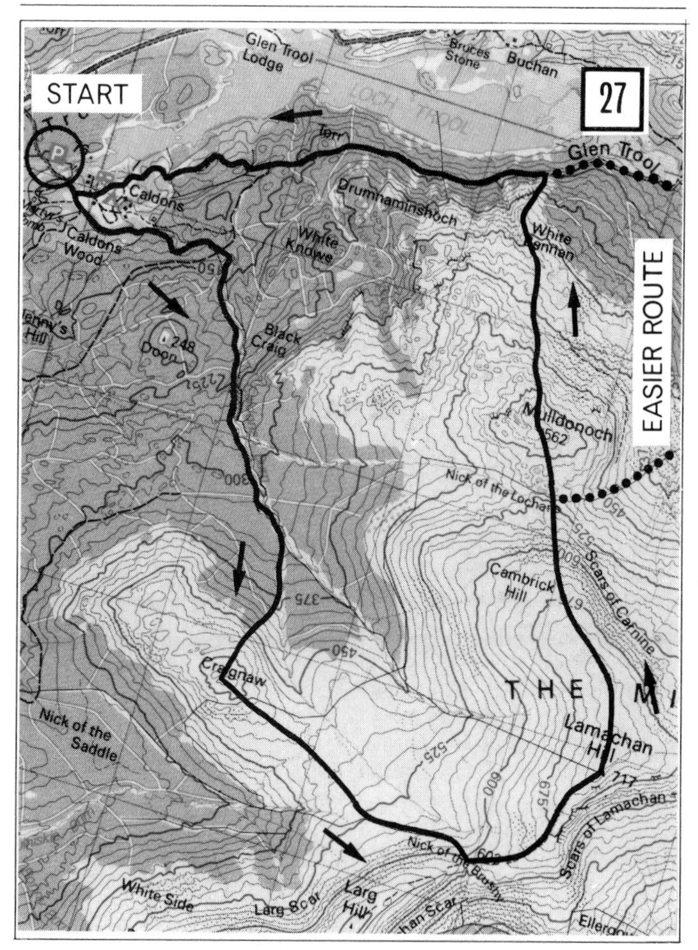

path can be muddy in places and you need to be careful above a steep-sided rocky gorge, which is full of waterfalls you'll hardly catch a glimpse of. As height is gained, you'll find that the trees of the forest are planted rather close to the water, so you may find it best to walk first on one bank and then on the other. However, be sure to look out for the tributary burn which branches off to the right, and follow that upstream to reach the edge of the forest. You can climb up a steep, grassy slope at the edge of the forest, then make a bid for the summit of Craignaw.

Follow the broad moorland crest away from Craignaw towards Larg Hill. There's a grassy and rocky descent and a fence to cross. As the slope levels out there's heather and bilberry to cross before a ruined wall is reached. Turn left to follow the wall across the slopes of Larg Hill, climbing to reach a gap called the Nick of the Brushy. The wall turns right at the gap to head for the summit of Larg Hill, but you should turn left and pick up a line of old metal fenceposts. These lead up the broad, grassy slopes of Lamachan Hill. There are odd large boulders dotted around the slopes, but the ascent is fairly gentle with no problems. There's an old wall running across the broad top of the hill which joins the line of old fenceposts at the 717m summit.

Head roughly northwards from the summit to cross the broad, flat, grassy top of the hill, but swing gradually to the left to keep on the broad crest and head for a solitary cairn. There's a good view towards the Range of the Awful Hand, the Dungeon Hills and the Rhinns of Kells. Continue along the crest to start descending Cambrick Hill. As the slope steepens the grass gets coarser and patches of bilberry and rock appear. Look ahead to gauge the best line down to the broad gap called the Nick of the Lochans. You'll be able to see a number of small pools on the boggy, hummocky gap - and there's a fence to be crossed too. If you wanted an easier end to this walk, then follow the fence off to the right down a rugged slope to land on a forest road below. Turn left to follow the forest road down into Glen Trool, following waymarks indicating the Southern Upland Way, to avoid the steep slopes of White Bennan.

Rising above the Nick of the Lochans, however, is a short, rugged pull up to the 562m summit cairn on Mulldonoch. There are rocky outcrops surrounding the summit area and a direct view down to Caldons Campsite where the walk started. Take care on the descent from Mulldonoch and look carefully for a sparsely cairned line down from the summit towards White Bennan. The terrain is pathless, but there are rocky outcrops and deep heather which is best avoided by following the cairned route. Once you're standing on the hump which forms the summit of White Bennan, there are superb views along Loch Trool and all around Glen Trool. The descent from this point towards the loch needs great care as it becomes very steep and rocky. Start the descent by heading off to the right, towards the head of Loch Trool. A blunt ridge runs steeply downhill and you'll notice a few stubbly trees further to the right. Now look off to the left to identify a steep gully full of grass and boulders, with a clear view down to the forest edge. Pick a careful way down the gully - on your backside with heels dug in if necessary! The boulders become difficult to cross just before the trees of the forest are reached, but press onwards through the trees to land on a clear path a short way into the forest.

The path is part of the Loch Trool Forest Trail and the Southern Upland Way. Turn left to follow it back to Caldons Campsite. A sign on the way explains how Robert the Bruce successfully ambushed an English force in 1307 by rolling boulders onto them. Later, you'll find a short side-spur from the trail at Torr which allows a view across Loch Trool to the distant bulk of Merrick. There are some minor switchbacks and in wet weather there may be muddy patches. There's a variety of trees with Scots pine giving way to oak cover near Caldons Campsite. Simply follow the campsite access road back to the car parks near the bridge. If you've time you might have a look at the Martyr's Tomb which is signposted nearby.

The Steps of Trool

This is another perspective on the Steps of Trool ambush site. From the top of White Bennan you can look directly down on the rugged slopes that the English crossed in 1307 under the leadership of Aymer de Valance. You can imagine yourself as one of Robert the Bruce's guerrilla fighters, with boulders poised ready to roll, while your comrades would be lying in wait to pick off any escapees with their arrows. From this vantage point you can also look over the Soldier's Holm, or Green Acre, where the dead were buried after the conflict at the head of Loch Trool.

⁂ ⁂ ⁂

The Soldier's Holm or Green Acre by Loch Trool's Head

WALK 28: CURLEYWEE AND LAMACHAN HILL FROM WHITE LAGGAN

The White Laggan Bothy is especially well placed for walkers who want to explore the Minnigaff Hills. Although the bothy offers only basic facilities - shelter from the elements and the option of a log fire - it can be used as a base and cuts out the need for long walk-ins every time you want to visit the surrounding hills. The walk described below starts and finishes at the bothy, but with an extension along a forest trail it could be made to start and finish at the Bruce's Stone at the head of Glen Trool. It could also be extended along a forest road in the other direction so that the start and finish would be at Craigencallie. The route covers the rugged hill of Curleywee and the tall, broad-shouldered Lamachan Hill. Mulldonoch is crossed on the descent, as well as its most northerly prow - White Bennan. You're being warned well in advance that the descent from the hills in that direction is very steep and difficult. It should not be attempted if there is snow, ice or frost on the ground. It was from those precipitous slopes that Robert the Bruce and his army ambushed a large English force, trundling boulders onto the

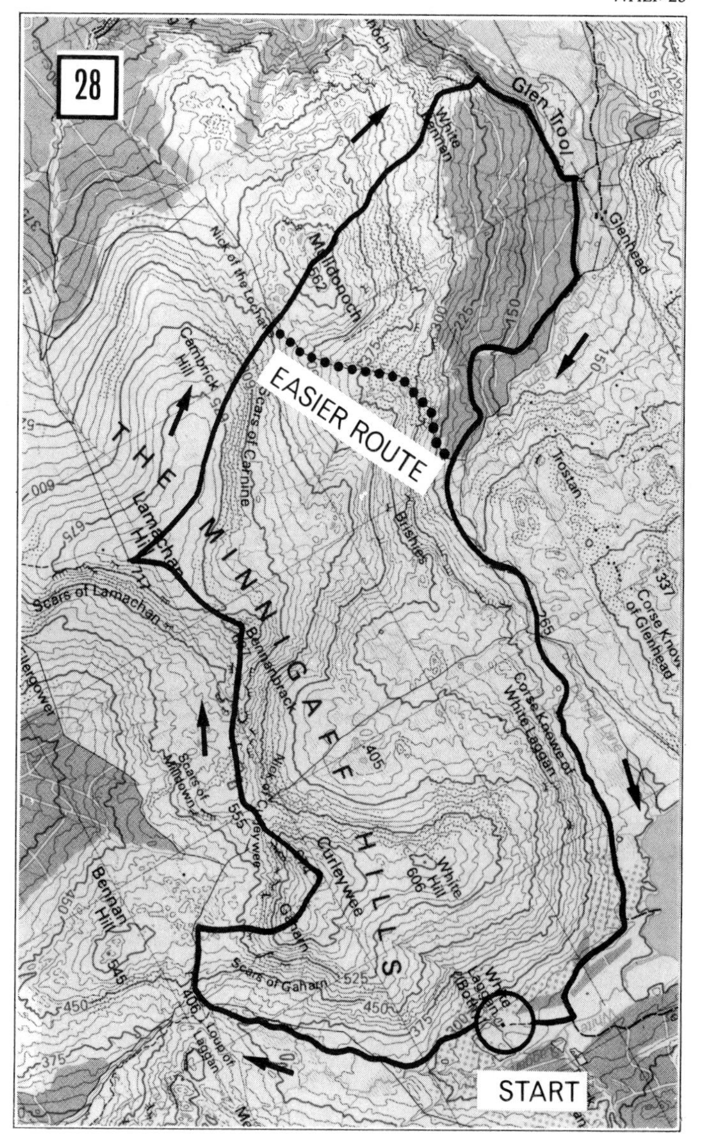
28
Glen Trool
Glenhead
White Bennan
Mulldonoch
562
Nick of the Lochans
Cambrick Hill
EASIER ROUTE
Scars of Cernine
THE MINNIGAFF HILLS
Lamachan Hill
717
Trostan
Brishie
Corse Knowe of Glenhead
337
Scars of Lamachan
Bennanbrack
Corse Knowe of White Laggan
405
Scars of Milldown
555
Curleywee
White Hill
606
Bennan Hill
545
Scars of Gaharn
525
Loup of Laggan
406
START

soldiers and successfully routing the army. There are superb views across Glen Trool in the middle of this walk, but if you think you could be struggling on the steep slopes, then consider taking the safer descent from the Nick of Lochans. Either way, the walk ends with a stretch of the long-distance Southern Upland Way to return to the bothy. The circuit offers views of the many faces of the Minnigaff Hills, from the summits to the lower slopes and from the forests to the bare hillsides.

The Route

Distance: A difficult hill walk of 10 miles (16km).

Start: At White Laggan Bothy - 467775.

Parking: For overnight parking use the Craigencallie car park.

Leave the White Laggan Bothy by walking up its nearby burn, crossing the burn, then following a clear, old road up into the valley. This is boggy in places, but always clearly in view ahead. There's a stile by a gate to be crossed to pass into a broad, boggy valley, then a gentle climb towards the head of the valley around the slopes of Curleywee. There's a gap at the head of the valley called the Loup of Laggan. It's not necessary to go all the way to the gap, as you can turn off to the right before that point and follow a fence up a rugged slope. This leads to a broad, boggy, hummocky gap. Another right turn takes you up a steep and rugged slope to the top of Curleywee. There's grass, heather and rock on this climb, but the ground levels out at Gaharn into a broad crest, with the summit cairn being reached at 674m just beyond. Enjoy the extensive views all around the Galloway Hills before moving on.

Descend roughly westwards to pick up the line of a steep, blunt ridge leading down to the Nick of Curleywee. There's a faint path leading down steeply on grass to that point. A fence and ruined wall have to be crossed, then you need to look out for a line of old metal fenceposts leading uphill. Follow these faithfully, usually to the left side of a hummocky, rocky ridge. The ridge leads up to a rocky hump called Bennanbrack at 687m. The fenceposts turn left at that point and lead up a gentle, grassy slope until a wall runs into them on the 717m summit of Lamachan Hill.

Head roughly northwards from the summit to cross the broad, flat, grassy top of the hill, but swing gradually to the left to keep on the broad crest and head for a solitary cairn. There's a good view towards the Range of the Awful Hand, the Dungeon Hills and the Rhinns of Kells. Continue along the crest to start descending Cambrick Hill. As the slope steepens the grass gets coarser and patches of bilberry and rock appear. Look ahead to gauge the best line down to the broad gap called the Nick of the Lochans. You'll be able to see a number of small pools on the boggy, hummocky gap - and there's a fence to be crossed too. If you wanted an easier end to this walk, then follow the fence off to the right down a rugged slope to land on a forest road below. Turn right to follow the forest road back round to White Laggan, following waymarks indicating the Southern Upland Way, to avoid the steep slopes of White Bennan.

Rising above the Nick of the Lochans, however, is a short, rugged pull up to the 562m summit cairn on Mulldonoch. There are rocky outcrops surrounding the summit area and a direct view down to Caldons Campsite is available. Take care on the descent from Mulldonoch and look carefully for a sparsely cairned line down from the summit towards White Bennan. The terrain is pathless, but there are rocky outcrops and deep heather which is best avoided by following the cairned route. Once you're standing on the hump which forms the summit of White Bennan, there are superb views along Loch Trool and all around Glen Trool. The descent from this point towards the loch needs great care as it becomes very steep and rocky. Start the descent by heading off to the right, towards the head of Loch Trool. A blunt ridge runs steeply downhill and you'll notice a few stubbly trees further to the right. Now look off to the left to identify a steep gully full of grass and boulders, with a clear view down to the forest edge. Pick a careful way down the gully. The boulders become difficult to cross just before the trees of the forest are reached, but press onwards through the trees to land on a clear path a short way into the forest.

The path is part of the Loch Trool Forest Trail and the Southern Upland Way. Turn right to follow the path towards the edge of the forest and gradually down into the glen at Glenhead Burn. The Southern Upland Way turns right just before a footbridge over the burn, and follows the burn upstream. The path eventually heads off uphill to the right and crosses a number of duckboards before emerging on a forest road. The forest road continues uphill to the left and eventually leaves the trees to pass through a wild valley. Simply follow the broad road over a rugged gap, where a stile by a gate is crossed, then continue around the lower slopes of Curleywee. There are views over Loch Dee before you reach a log-pile by the roadside. Collect an armful of logs and carry them up to the White Laggan Bothy for fuel.

The White Laggan Bothy

White Laggan and Black Laggan were neighbouring farms, but as hard times fell on the area their inhabitants moved out. White Laggan was vacated and fell into ruins first, with Black Laggan being vacated later. Curiously, however, it was White Laggan which was restored as a bothy. Basic accommodation is offered, with two rooms downstairs and a small room known as the "kitchen" off to one side. Upstairs is a room under the roof which overlooks the one room downstairs which has a fireplace. There's enough room in the bothy for a small group of walkers, but the place can be quite popular and crowds easily. It is used not only by casual walkers, fishermen and foresters, but is the only accommodation for quite a distance on the Southern Upland Way. Logs are usually sawn and chopped beside the forest road nearby, so all you usually need to do is carry them up the path from the road to the bothy for a fire.

* * *

WALK 29: CRAIGLEE AND LOCH DEE FROM WHITE LAGGAN

The Dungeon Hills are the most rugged and rocky of the Galloway Hills, being surrounded sometimes by boilerplate slabs and buttresses of granite, or scattered with ill-sorted boulders and clothed in tough grass and heather with boggy patches and scores of little lochans. It's generally difficult walking country, and you need to be a good navigator in poor visibility, but it's a great wilderness area to savour to the utmost. The walk over Craiglee is perhaps easier than other walks in the Dungeon Hills. You could approach Craiglee from either Glen Trool or from the Craigencallie road, but you can cut out the walk-in if you're based at the White Laggan Bothy. Easy forest roads are followed at the beginning and

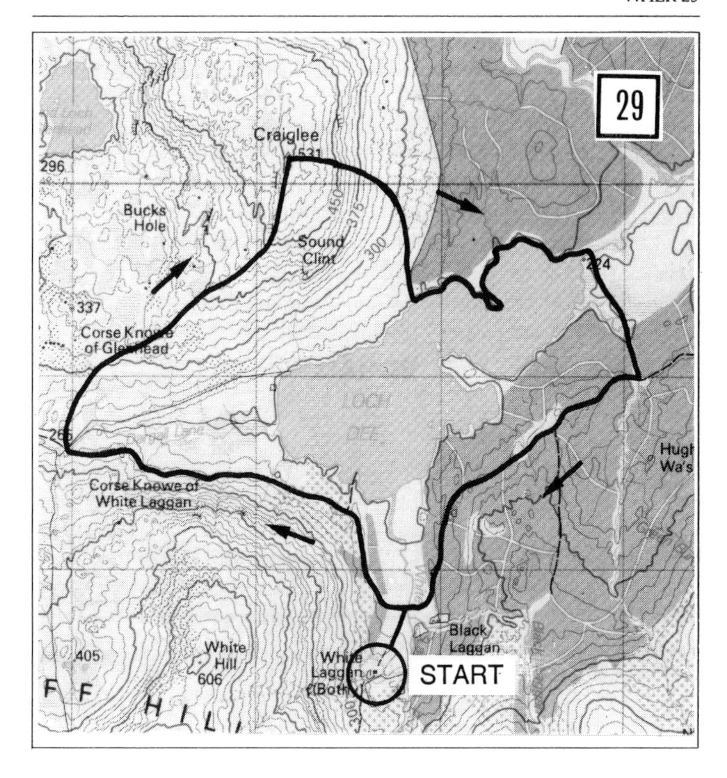

end of the walk - part of the Southern Upland Way - though the walk over Craiglee is quite rugged.

The Route

Distance:	A difficult hill walk of $7^1/_2$ miles (12km).
Start:	At White Laggan Bothy - 467775.
Parking:	For overnight parking use the Craigencallie car park.

Walk down the boggy path from the White Laggan Bothy and turn left to follow the forest road around the lower slopes of Curleywee. The road is part of the Southern Upland Way and leads to a rugged gap where there's a stile by a gate. Turn right immediately and go through a gate in a fence to reach the open slopes of Craiglee. You can choose any line which you consider reasonable to reach the top. You could start making height straight away on the Corse Knowe of Glenhead, then swing to the right along the broad, boggy, rocky crest of the hill. You'll have to pick your way round squelchy patches and outcrops of rock, crossing tussocky grass and heather. As height is gained, some small, sheer cliffs become apparent. One line of these can be followed practically to the summit, either by walking along the foot of the cliff, or keeping to a blunt ridge above it. The summit of Craiglee is a dome of granite bearing a trig point at 531m, with views into the rugged and rocky heart of the Dungeon Hills.

A descent can be made almost directly eastwards, though you need to avoid small outcrops of rock at first. The ground steepens quickly and the slope is roughly vegetated. There's no great obstacle on this descent and when the slope begins to run out at the bottom of the hill you can swing off to the right and aim for a point where a forest fence reaches the shore of Loch Dee. Cross the fence and follow the shore faithfully - even to the extent of going round all the little headlands and bays. There are beaches of coarse, white sand and eventually you'll reach the outflow. A footbridge crosses the river and a vague path leads away from it towards the nearby forest. The path runs alongside a small burn and climbs gently to reach a forest road. Turn right to walk along the road, which is also used by the Southern Upland Way, until you reach a log-pile by the roadside. Collect an armful of logs and carry them up to the White Laggan Bothy for fuel.

* * *

WALK 30: CRAIGLEE FROM CRAIGENCALLIE

Craiglee occupies a fairly central position in the Galloway Hills, so it can be approached from a number of directions. It is one of the Dungeon Hills, so the ground is very rugged and pathless, though it's probably fair to say that Craiglee is the easiest of the Dungeon Hills to climb. The walk offered below starts from Craigencallie and makes use of a lengthy forest road at first, part of which is used by the Southern Upland Way. After passing Loch Dee, a direct ascent can be made to the summit of Craiglee. A very rugged descent is

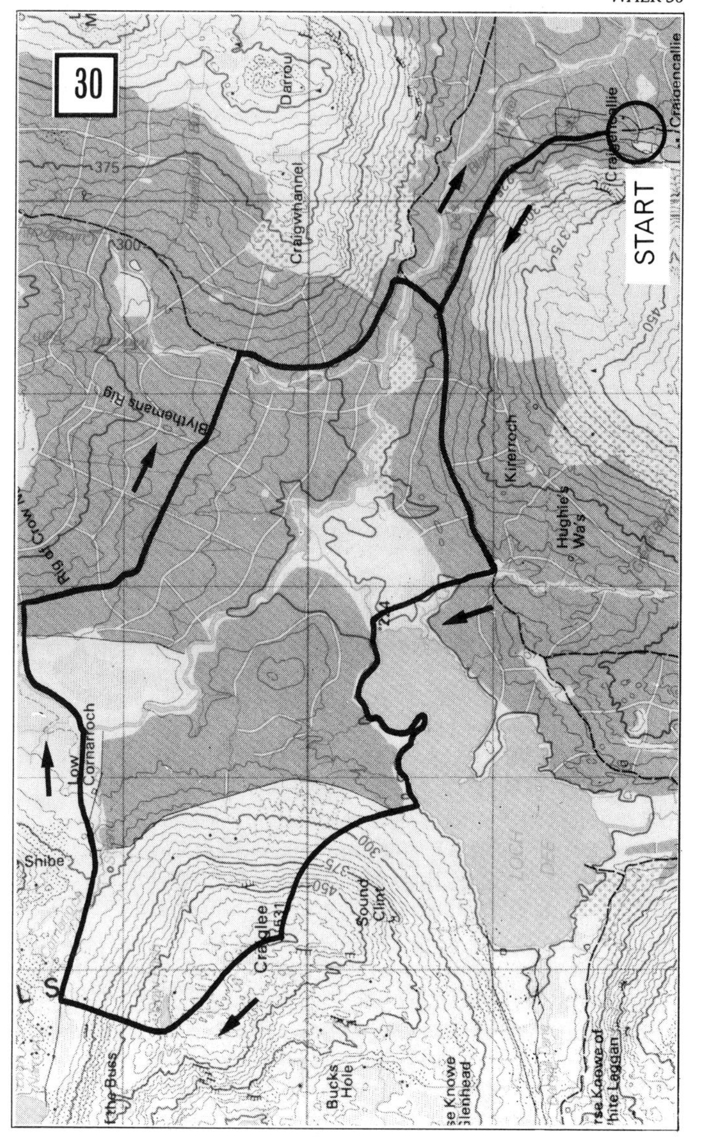
30
START
Craigencallie
Darrou
Craigwhannel
Blythemans Rig
Kirerroch
Hughie's
Wa's
Low
Cornarroch
Shibe
Craiglee
631
Sound
Clint
Bucks
Hole
300
375
450

followed by a walk across the boggy levels of the Silver Flow. A forest road allows a simple walk-out to Craigencallie. With some amendment to the route this walk could be attempted from bases such as the White Laggan or the Backhill of Bush Bothy.

The Route

Distance: A difficult hill walk of 10 miles (16km).

Start: At Craigencallie - 504781.

Parking: By the forest road gate at Craigencallie.

Leave the little roadside car park at Craigencallie and go over the stile by the gate on the forest road. The road keeps low on the slopes of Cairnarroch at first, then you turn off to the left at a junction of forests road to follow part of the Southern Upland Way. The forest road rises gently, then descends gently to a point where a small burn goes under the road. Turn right off the road and walk alongside the burn. A vague path leads to a footbridge over the outflow from Loch Dee. Cross the bridge and turn left to follow the shore of the loch faithfully, going around all the little headlands and bays. There are beaches of coarse white sand and you continue as far as a forest fence before turning away from the loch shore. The slopes of Craiglee are roughly vegetated, but there's no great obstacle barring a way to the summit. Start climbing gradually across the flank of the hill, then swing round to aim more directly for the top, avoiding any small outcrops of rock on the way. The summit of Craiglee is a dome of granite bearing a trig point at 531m, with views into the rugged and rocky heart of the Dungeon Hills.

Descend by heading roughly north-westwards along the gently sloping, but rugged crest of the hill. There is bare rock, boulders and pools of water to pass. Look out for the lovely Dow Loch which nestles in a rocky little notch on the ridge. You can head off to the right and pick a careful way down the steep, rugged slopes of the hill. There is plenty of grass, heather and bilberry with rocks slowing the descent. There's a fence at the foot of the slope and you should cross it before turning right to follow it roughly parallel to the course of Cornarroch Strand. There's a lot of boggy ground covered in tussocky grass, but the fence offers a sure guide across the Silver Flow to reach Cooran Lane. Turn left to follow Cooran

The stony Curleywee above the Nick of Curleywee

Looking along the length of Loch Trool and Glen Trool

Looking along the River Dee to the hump of Craiglee
Walking across the strange De'ils Bowling Green

Lane upstream. The river is very deep in places, but you should be able to cross it at a rocky part. Once across, continue upstream until you reach a sign. From the sign, aim for the nearby forest, looking for a ride which leads between the trees. A rather messy forest ride runs from the edge of the forest through to a firm forest road near the Rig of Crow Nest. Turn right to follow the forest road until it crosses Curnelloch Burn, then turn right again to swing round the lower slopes of Craigwhannel. You'll reach a large, triangular junction of forest roads and you should turn right again to cross the River Dee. As the road leads uphill, make a left turn to walk back to the car park under the frowning face of Craigencallie.

The Silver Flow

"Flow" or "Flowe" is a term used to describe a great tract of low, level, wet ground vegetated with rough grasses. The Silver Flow is hemmed in between the Dungeon Hills and the Rhinns of Kells, and it slopes almost imperceptibly southwards. The best views of it are from the Dungeon Hills, while the worst place to be is in the middle of it. A couple of sheepfolds have been built on the Flow, but it offers only poor grazing and these days it has been left to grow into a semi-wild state. It is managed as a National Nature Reserve and has a typical bogland flora, as well as offering good cover for nesting birds. It has largely been spared from the blanket afforestation that has afflicted other hills and valleys in the area. The only routes in this guide which impinge on the Flow follow either fences or rivers, and no routes go straight across its complex, boggy middle reaches. You would notice, from on high on a sunny day, that it's pock-marked with pools of water and some parts are "quaking" bog which can prove dangerous to cross. In recent years, the Flow was partly ablaze, with the fire spreading into the young plantation near Cornarroch Strand, as well as spreading across the slopes of Craignaw to Loch Valley. The ground seems to be recovering, but only time will tell if the flora and fauna become re-established in the proportions previously noted.

⁂ ⁂ ⁂

WALK 31: LOCH VALLEY AND CRAIGLEE FROM GLEN TROOL

Craiglee may be one of the easiest of the Dungeon Hills to climb, but it is nevertheless a very rugged hill. Slabs of granite characterise these hills, with boulders scattered all over the boggy ground and roughly vegetated terrain. Small lochans abound, while the larger lochs have incredibly complicated shorelines. In fact, you may sometimes think you're looking at the full expanse of some of these lochs, only to find later that you've only been looking at a small part. The Dungeon Hills form the wild heartland of the Galloway Hills and normally you'd expect to have to make a long walk-in. Craiglee, however, can be approached from a number of directions. On this walk, the hill is reached using the Loch Valley path from the head of Glen Trool. After the rugged climb you can descend to the Southern Upland Way and let it take you back down into the glen.

The Route

Distance: A difficult hill walk of 8½ miles (14km).

Start: At the Bruce's Stone - 415804.

Parking: At the car park by the Bruce's Stone.

Park at the end of the Glen Trool road, close to the Bruce's Stone. If the last space is full, then park just before at another car park by a toilet block. Follow the rough road down from the car park into a small oakwood. The road crosses Buchan Bridge, which was "designed and executed by Randolph IX Earl of Galloway AD 1851". There's also a verse carved in stone and a little waterfall to admire. A little further along the road, on the left, is a sign for Gairland Burn and Loch Valley. Cross a stile and follow a path up through fields. The path follows a wall at first, then drifts away from it. When it comes back alongside the wall, go through a small swing gate. The path leads across a bracken-clad slope and turns into a valley. As the bracken runs out, the path continues across a grassy slope and gradually moves closer to Gairland Burn as it follows the burn upstream. Some parts at the head of the valley can be boggy and muddy, but boulders make good stepping stones in the worst parts.

Cross over Gairland Burn when you reach Loch Valley, then

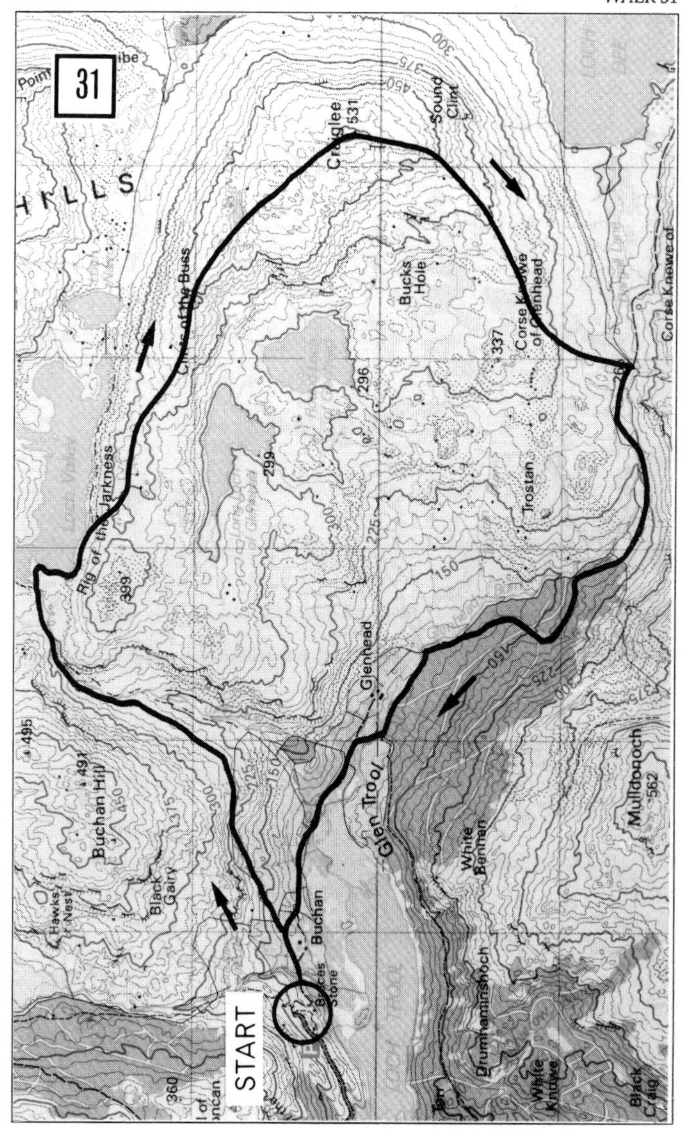
31
START
HILLS
Craiglee
531
Sound Clint
Cliffs of the Buss
Rig of the Jarkness
399
296
299
337
Bucks Hole
Corse Knowe of Glenhead
Trostan
Glenhead
Glen Trool
White Bennan
Mulldonoch
562
Buchan Hill
491
495
Black Gairy
Hawks Nest
Buchan
Stone
White Knowe
Black Craig
360

follow a very vague shoreline path. There are rugged slopes falling into the loch, clothed in grass, heather, bilberry and boulders. You should climb this difficult slope, which leads up to the broad Rig of the Jarkness. Keep to this broad crest, which is all tussocky grass, heather and boulders as it climbs to the Clints of the Buss. As you struggle ever upwards, look out for the lovely Dow Loch which nestles in a rocky little notch in the ridge. There isn't much more climbing to reach the top of Craiglee, but it's still rough country with more and more granite exposed. The summit is a dome of granite bearing a trig point at 531m, with views into the rugged and rocky heart of the Dungeon Hills.

Descend roughly southwards from the summit at first. You can either stay on a blunt ridge, or keep more to the right and trace the foot of a sheer cliff downhill. Either way, you'll have to drift off to the right towards the Corse Knowe of Glenhead. The descent involves picking a way around squelchy patches and outcrops of rock, crossing tussocky grass and heather. As the gradient levels out in a hummocky area, head off to the left down a rugged, boggy slope to reach a forest road. A gate in a fence gives access to the road, then you turn right and follow it down a wild valley to enter a forest. This line is also used by the Southern Upland Way. The forest road runs down into the forest, then later there's a path off to the right which runs down towards Glenhead Burn. This path is surfaced with duckboards in places, then runs downstream alongside the burn. When you reach a footbridge, cross over it and turn left. After a short while, turn right as indicated by the green markers of the Loch Trool Forest Trail. The path leads to the access road for Glenhead, where you turn left away from the farmstead. The road crosses Buchan Bridge and enters a small oakwood as at the beginning of the day's walk. Simply follow the rough road back up to the car park near the Bruce's Stone.

* * *

WALK 32: THE DUNGEON HILLS FROM BACKHILL OF BUSH

One way to avoid a lengthy walk-in to the Dungeon Hills is to use the Backhill of Bush Bothy as a base. The bothy could accommodate a small walking group and give them shelter from the elements, as

Dungeon Hill's rocky face and smooth Corserine

well as having both a stove and fireplace, and a supply of logs. The bothy faces the forbiddingly rugged Dungeon Hills, which exhibit boilerplate slabs and soaring buttresses which make the whole range seem almost unassailable. Access to the range is also barred with a strip of forestry, beyond which are a deep river and the awesome boggy levels of the Silver Flow. Amazingly, even with all those apparent obstacles stacked against you, it's still possible to reach the Dungeon Hills without too much difficulty. You need to be a good navigator in poor visibility on the Dungeon Hills, as it's easy to go seriously wrong in a rather confusing landscape of boulders, rocky outcrops, pools of water and bogs.

The Route

Distance: A difficult hill walk of 9 miles (15km).

Start: At Backhill of Bush Bothy - 481843.

Parking: For overnight parking use the Craigencallie car park.

Leave the Backhill of Bush Bothy and cross over the nearby forest road to follow a forest ride through to Saugh Burn. You'll need to cross Saugh Burn to reach the boggy ground of the Silver Flow and you should ford the river almost immediately and turn right. Follow the river upstream until you reach the forest fence, then turn left. It's quite heavy going over the squelchy, tussocky grass, but the forest fence is a sure guide gently uphill. When the fence turns a corner to the right, you could branch away from it and walk across the rugged, lower slopes of the Dungeon Hills - at least until you've passed Dry Loch on the rugged moorland gap. You'll start drifting downhill from Dry Loch, but before long you should be looking for a very vague path ascending across the slope on the left. This leads up the slopes of Brishie at a fairly gentle angle and turns around the blunt end of the ridge, where you can leave it for a more direct ascent. The ridge is steep and rocky in places, but it levels out further up and takes you onwards towards the top of Dungeon Hill. There is a cairn on the 620m summit of the hill and a good view down onto the Silver Flow, as well as all round the surrounding hills.

All around Dungeon Hill is a desolate scene of bog and boulders, with great slabs of granite tilting towards fearsome cliffs. Head roughly westwards from the summit to reach a broad gap, but you'll have to switch this way and that to avoid huge benches of rock and pools of water. A short, gently graded, but very rugged slope leads up to the 595m summit of Craignairny. A southerly course leads down from the summit to the Nick of the Dungeon. On this downhill stretch, it's possible to walk down broad ribs of granite instead of threading a way between outcropping rock. The ribs have a good angle and friction, but you still need to be careful not to slip. The way down seems reasonable while you're on the rock, but when you look back up the slope from the bottom it looks quite difficult. There's a cairn on the gap, as well as grass, heather and small pools. Start climbing up the next slope, using a vague path if you can spot it. You'll find yourself walking over a huge dome of granite surrounded by slabs and ledges of rock. The whole place is scattered with ill-sorted boulders. One large, tilted slab full of boulders is known as the De'ils Bowling Green. Almost straight ahead at that point is a steep face cut by a narrow defile of rock and heather. You'll find that many walkers before you have used this breach to gain the 645m summit of Craignaw. There is a cairn on top, surrounded by great rounded outcrops of granite, with superb

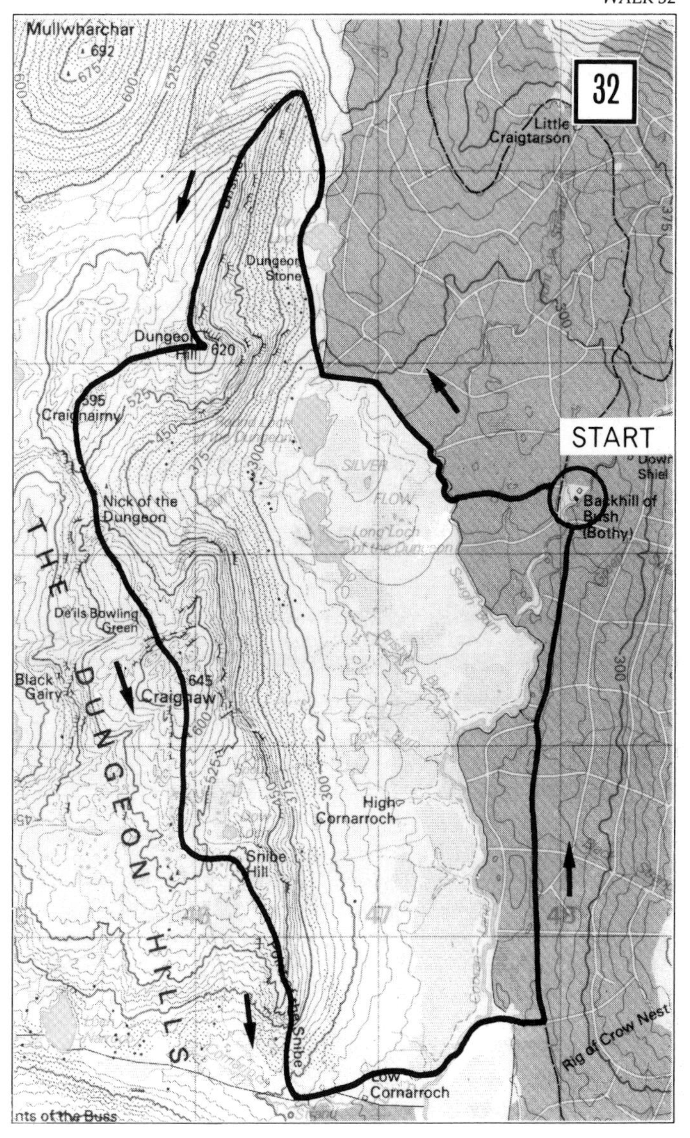

32
START
Mullwharchar
692
Little Craigtarson
Dungeon Stone
Dungeon Hill
620
595
Craignairny
SILVER FLOW
Long Loch of the Dungeon
Nick of the Dungeon
THE DUNGEON HILLS
De'ils Bowling Green
Black Gairy
645
Craignaw
Backhill of Bush (Bothy)
High Cornarroch
Snibe Hill
Low Cornarroch
Rig of Crow Nest
nts of the Buss

views of the surrounding hills.

The descent southwards along a broad crest involves picking a way round rocky outcrops, passing patches of heather, grass and boggy bits, until you can swing leftwards towards the rugged excrescence of Snibe Hill. Try to avoid going down to Dow Loch and stay on the broad, stony crest to pass small pools to reach Snibe Hill. Again, head roughly southwards along the Point of the Snibe, but don't walk straight off the end of it. Instead, before reaching the rocky end of the ridge, you should head off to the left down a steep and rugged slope overlooking the Silver Flow. Pick a way past tough vegetation and avoid outcrops of rock, but aim towards Cornarroch Strand rather than the level boggy ground of the Silver Flow. As the slope eases, the long grass becomes very tussocky and the walk towards Cornarroch Strand is quite difficult underfoot.

There's a fence running roughly parallel to the course of Cornarroch Strand, and a lot of boggy ground covered in tussocky grass. The fence offers a sure guide across the Silver Flow to reach Cooran Lane. Turn left to follow Cooran Lane upstream. The river is very deep in places, but you should able to cross it at a rocky part. Once across, continue upstream until you reach a sign. From the sign, aim for the nearby forest, looking for a ride which leads between the trees. A rather messy forest ride runs from the edge of the forest through to a firm forest road near the Rig of Crow Nest. Turn left to follow the forest road back towards the Backhill of Bush Bothy, which is eventually seen across a clearing on the right of the road after crossing Downies Burn.

The De'ils Bowling Green

The story goes that the Devil and the goat-god Pan simply couldn't decide who was going to eat a loaf of bread, and with their hunger pangs growing they reached a novel solution. They decided to play a game of bowls and the winner would have the loaf of bread. A flat slab of granite served as the playing area and heaps of rounded boulders were gathered to serve as bowls. Unfortunately, as the game progressed there were accusations of cheating and the upshot was that they ended up hurling boulders at each other. Hence, the scene you see before you today - the flat slab with the unfinished game of bowls still on it and the surrounding hills covered in boulders. As for the loaf of bread, well, just to the north-west of the summit of Craignaw is a hump of granite known as the De'ils Loaf!

❊ ❊ ❊

WALK 33: THE DUNGEON HILLS FROM GLEN TROOL

One of the most difficult and entertaining day's walks in the Galloway Hills is found right in the middle of the wilderness. A circuit taking in the Dungeon Hills and a number of weirdly-shaped lochs in that desolate tract of country is most interesting. The easiest way to link into such a circuit is by following the Loch Valley path from the Bruce's Stone at the head of Glen Trool. It's also possible to attempt the walk from bases such as the White Laggan Bothy or the Backhill of Bush Bothy. You could walk in from Craigencallie or even Loch Doon, but these would be very long approaches. Spare a thought for Robert the Bruce, caught between two advancing armies in that remote fastness, having to flee for his life when all and sundry were out for the bounty on his head.

The Route

Distance:	A difficult hill walk of 11 miles (18km).
Start:	At the Bruce's Stone - 415804.
Parking:	At the car park by the Bruce's Stone.

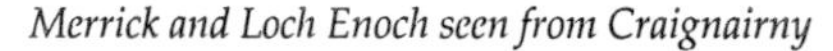

Merrick and Loch Enoch seen from Craignairny

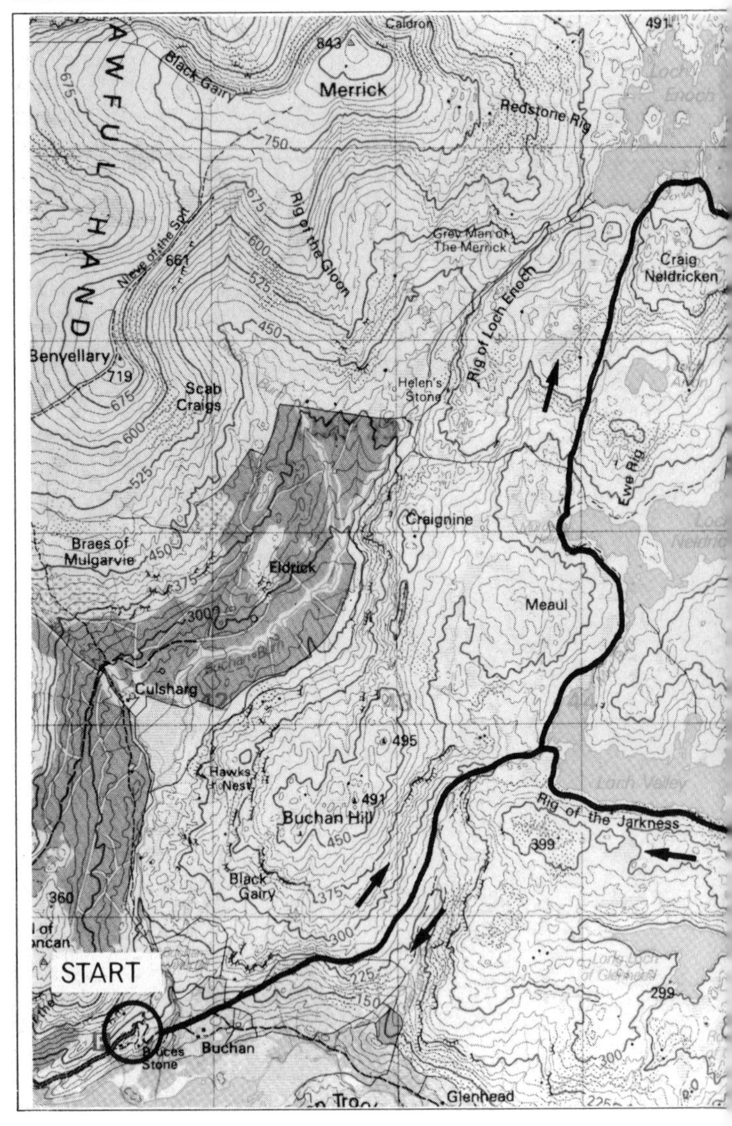
AWFUL HAND
Caldron
843
Merrick
Black Gairy
491
Loch Enoch
Redstone Rig
750
675
Rig of the Gloon
Grey Man of The Merrick
Nieve of the Spit
661
600
525
Craig Neldricken
Rig of Loch Enoch
450
Benyellary
719
Scab Craigs
Helen's Stone
Ewe Rig
Braes of Mulgarvie
Craignine
Eldrick
375
300
Meaul
Culsharg
495
Hawks Nest
491
Rig of the Jarkness
Buchan Hill
399
Black Gairy
360
225
START
299
150
Bruces Stone
Buchan
Glenhead

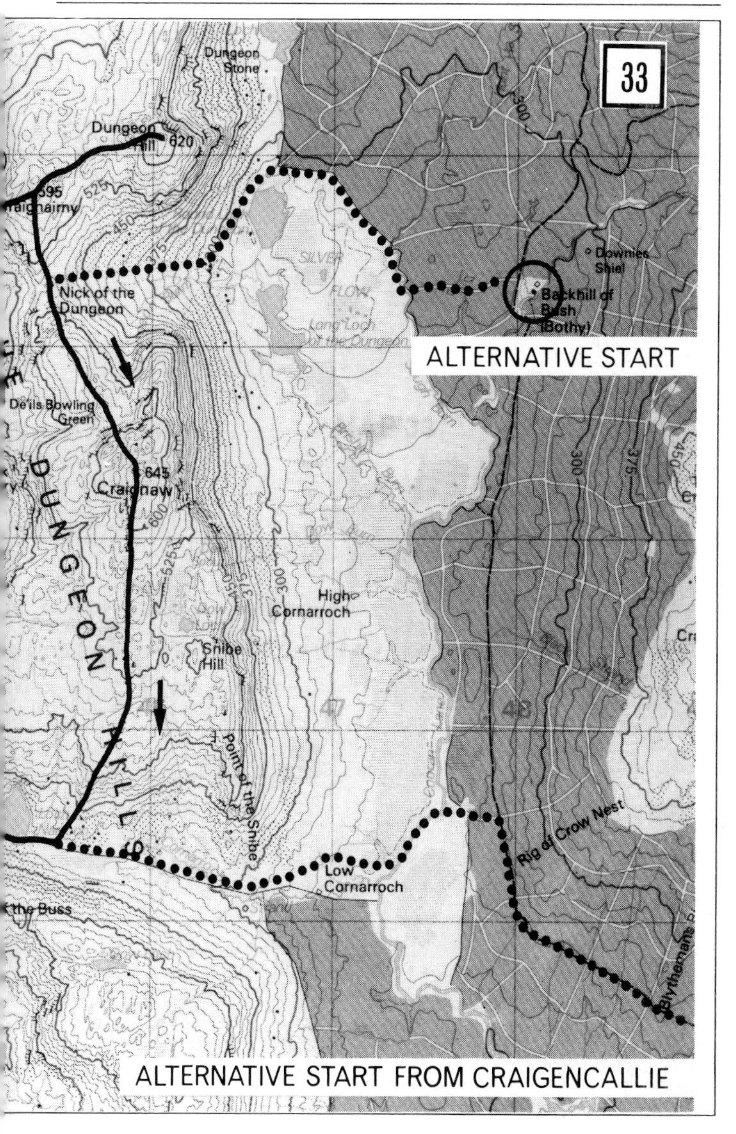
33
Dungeon Stone
Dungeon Hill
620
595
Craignairny
525
450
375
Nick of the Dungeon
SILVER
FLOW
Long Loch of the Dungeon
Downies Shiel
Backhill of Bush (Bothy)
300
ALTERNATIVE START
De'ils Bowling Green
645
Craignaw
600
525
DUNGEON HILL
300
375
450
High Cornarroch
Snibe Hill
Point of the Snibe
47
48
Rig of Crow Nest
Low Cornarroch
the Buss
Blythemans
ALTERNATIVE START FROM CRAIGENCALLIE

Park at the end of the Glen Trool road, close to the Bruce's Stone. If this last space is full, then park just before at another car park by a toilet block. Follow the rough road down from the car park into a small oakwood. The road crosses Buchan Bridge, which was "designed and executed by Randolph IX Earl of Galloway AD 1851". There's also a verse carved in stone and a little waterfall to admire. A little further along the road, on the left, is a sign for Gairland Burn and Loch Valley. Cross a stile and follow a path up through fields. The path follows a wall at first, then drifts away from it. When it comes back alongside the wall, go through a small swing-gate. The path leads across a bracken-clad slope and turns into a valley. As the bracken runs out, the path continues across a grassy slope and gradually moves closer to Gairland Burn as it follows the burn upstream. Some parts at the head of the valley can be boggy and muddy, but boulders make good stepping stones in the worst parts.

Walk roughly northwards along the shore of Loch Valley, crossing boggy ground covered in grass and heather. Mid Burn tumbles down across bare rock and boulders and you'll pass an old sheepfold while following the burn upstream to Loch Neldricken. The southern end of the loch is clogged with weeds, and as you follow the path around the shore you'll notice how shallow the water is in many places. Numerous rocks peep above the surface of the water. The boggy path around the shore finally passes a little bay known as the Murder Hole. Beyond that point you cross a ruined wall and follow the path uphill through a small valley. There are squelchy areas of bog and some places scattered around with boulders. If you keep an eye peeled you'll notice Loch Arron off to the right, though you don't walk out to it. Keep walking uphill and across a little gap to descend to a bay on the shore of Loch Enoch.

Turn right to start walking around the shore of Loch Enoch. You don't need to go round every bay and headland, but you can admire the beaches of coarse white sand. There's also some aircraft wreckage scattered around. Some parts adjoining the shore are boggy, but eventually you'll cross a fence and start climbing uphill. It's not too rough an ascent, but there are rocky outcrops and patches of tough grass and heather on the way up Craignairny. A cairn marks the 595m summit. It's worth heading down a little to the north-east to cross a very rugged gap and detour to the 620m summit of Dungeon Hill - simply for the view. You'll have to pick a careful way back to the top of Craignairny to continue with the circuit.

A southerly course leads down from the summit to the Nick of the Dungeon. On this downhill stretch, it's possible to walk down broad ribs of granite instead of threading a way between outcropping rock. The ribs have a good angle and friction, but you still need to be careful not to slip. The way down seems reasonable while you're on the rock, but when you look back up the slope from the bottom it looks quite difficult. There's a cairn on the gap, as well as grass, heather and small pools. Start climbing up the next slope, using a vague path if you can spot it. You'll find yourself walking over a huge dome of granite surrounded by slabs and ledges of rock. The whole place is scattered with ill-sorted boulders. One large, tilted slab full of boulders is known as the De'ils Bowling Green. Almost straight ahead at that point is a steep face cut by a narrow defile of rock and heather. You'll find that many walkers before you have used this breach to gain the 645m summit of Craignaw. There is a cairn on top, surrounded by great rounded outcrops of granite, with superb views of the surrounding hills.

The descent southwards along a broad crest involves picking a way round rocky outcrops, passing patches of heather, grass and boggy bits, until you can walk straight towards a couple of prominent cairns. Passing these, continue across a broad and desolate area which gradually steepens near Loch Narroch. Carefully pick a way down this final slope, crossing tough vegetation and outflanking rocky outcrops, When you reach a fence at the bottom, turn right and follow it. You'll pass Loch Narroch and soon be walking along the southern shore of Loch Valley. Despite a faint path, this is all rugged country with boulders scattered throughout the heather, grass and bilberry. When you find Gairland Burn flowing out of Loch Valley, cross it and turn left to follow it downstream. The path by Gairland Burn was used at the start of the day's walk and you simply follow it down to lower fields near Buchan and follow the rough road back towards the Bruce's Stone and the car park.

Robert the Bruce in the Dungeon Hills

Robert the Bruce was near Loch Enoch with his small force when Aymer de Valance was seen closing in on them from the north with a number of Highlanders in his army. Fleeing southwards to escape, the Bruce and his men found John of Lorn advancing from Glen Trool. Realising he might be caught in a pincer movement, the Bruce split his force into three and sent everyone off in different directions to confuse his pursuers. Unfortunately, John of Lorn had a bloodhound which had once belonged to Robert the Bruce and this led the soldiers towards their quarry. The Bruce sent all his men away except for his foster brother and they tried to outrun the hound. John of Lorn sent five burly Highlanders after them to try and delay their flight. All five were slain, but the bloodhound was gaining on the Bruce, leading the pursuers down from the Nick of the Dungeon.

Although exhausted after fighting the Highlanders, the Bruce and his foster brother crossed the boggy Silver Flow and waded and swam down Cooran Lane to throw off the hound. In some tales, the foster brother is said to have doubled back and put an arrow through the dog. Cold, wet and hungry, the two men came across three men who were carrying a sheep which they intended to cook. They said that they wanted to join Robert the Bruce's army, but something about their bearing suggested that they more likely wanted his head. The sheep was killed and eaten below the Rhinns of Kells, but as the Bruce slept that night he was woken by the three men advancing on him. Although his foster brother was slain almost instantly, the Bruce put the lot of them to death in the ensuing fight. Afterwards, he made his way to Craigencallie to await the reappearance of his little army.

Longer Walks

The last few walks in this guide are longer, harder walks. They range from a low-level route through forestry plantations to a series of difficult one-day walks which cross entire ranges of hills. Also offered below is a Grand Tour which would take up to five days to complete as it traverses most of the high ground in the area. The Southern Upland Way has been mentioned in some of the day walks, so a note explains a bit more about this long-distance route. Although only brief notes are offered about each of these longer walks, you'll find that practically all the ground covered on them is described in greater depth in the day walks list from 1 to 33.

WALK 34: THE FOREST WALK

Distance: 30 miles (48km).

Start: Stroan Bridge - 371786.

Finish: Stinchar Bridge - 387957.

This is a low-level route entirely along forest roads, paths or rides. Strong walkers could complete it in a day, but it might be better to split it over two days. It starts at the Glen Trool Visitor Centre and ends at Stinchar Bridge. There are a couple of handy bothies along the way where you could break the journey. You start by following an easy waymarked trail from Stroan Bridge alongside the Water of Trool to pass Caldons Campsite. The trail is also used by the Southern Upland Way and you continue along the rugged, southern side of Loch Trool almost to Glenhead. There is a path which leads up to a forest road, then the road leaves the forest to cross a rugged, open gap in the hills. The White Laggan Bothy offers basic accommodation a short way off-route near Loch Dee. The forest road and Southern Upland Way stay on the forested slopes above Loch Dee, then when the road crosses the River Dee the Southern Upland Way heads off to the right. Turn left at that point, then left again around the forested slopes of Craigeazle. The road runs close

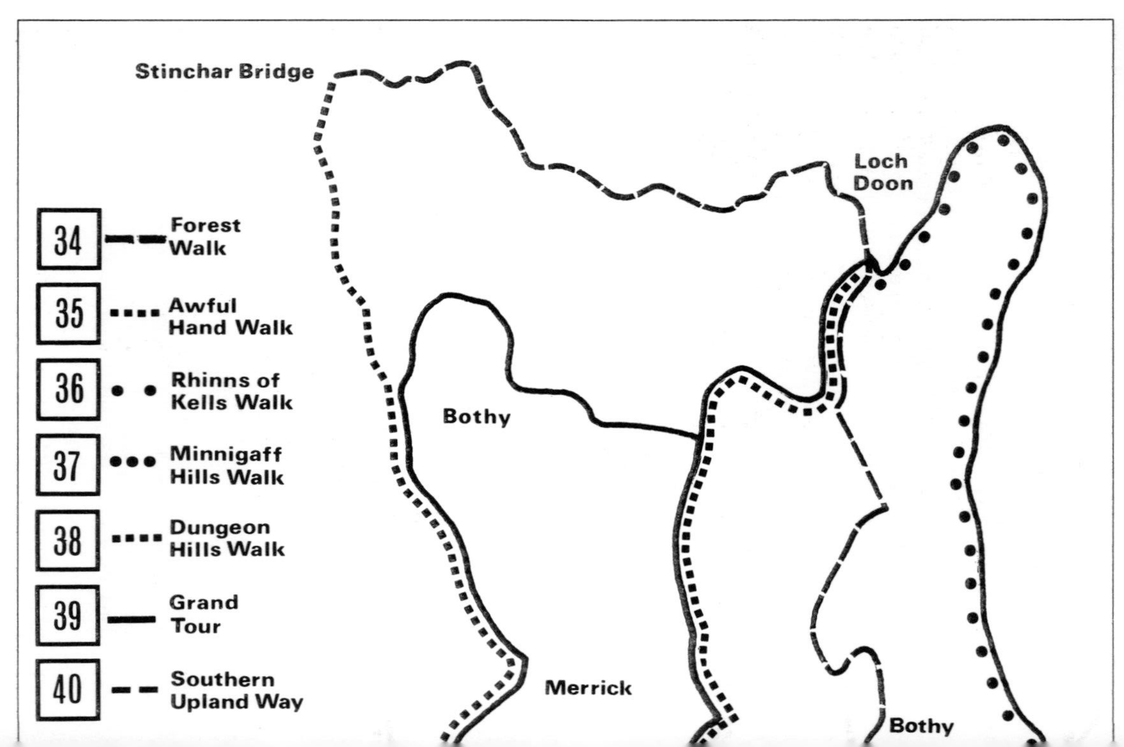
Stinchar Bridge
Loch Doon
34 Forest Walk
35 Awful Hand Walk
36 Rhinns of Kells Walk
37 Minnigaff Hills Walk
38 Dungeon Hills Walk
39 Grand Tour
40 Southern Upland Way
Bothy
Merrick
Bothy

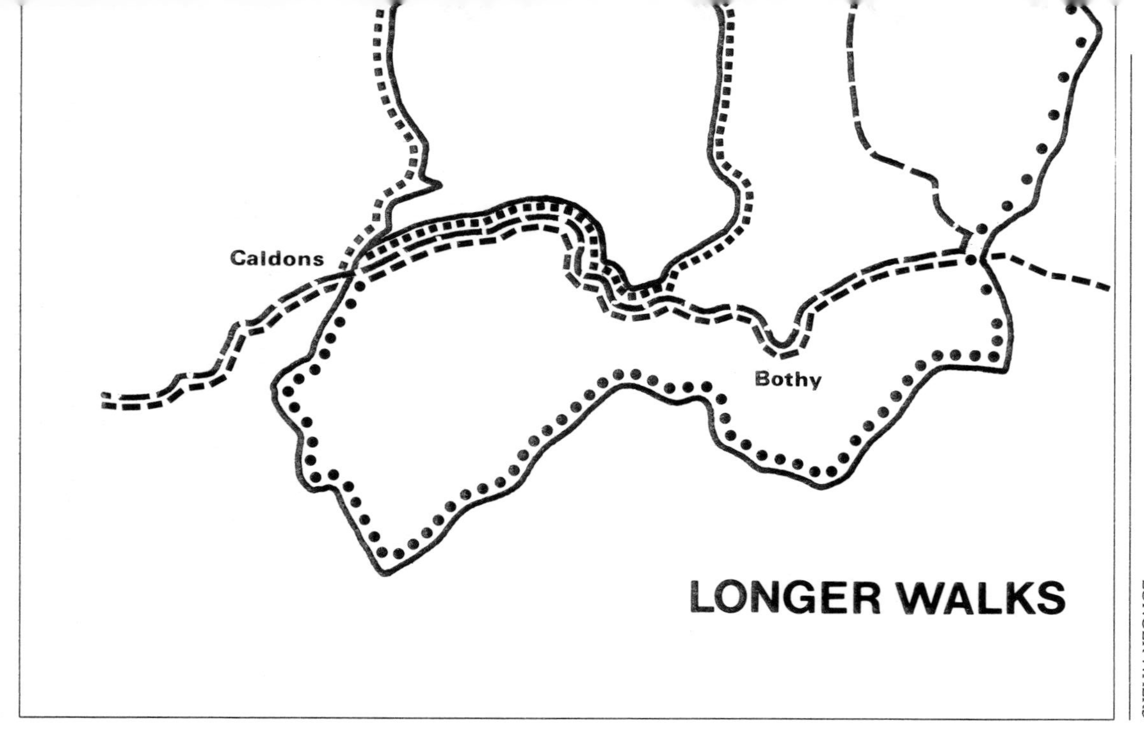
Caldons
Bothy
LONGER WALKS

to the Backhill of Bush Bothy, which is conveniently situated at the half-way mark on this walk.

You follow the forest road almost to its end, but branch off to the left at a stout post and fire beaters. A ride runs across Kirreoch Burn and tussocky grass has to be crossed before you land on a forest road. Turn right to follow this road almost to the head of Loch Doon. Turn left and follow another road across Gala Lane and Carrick Lane to reach the start of the Carrick Forest Drive. A left turn takes you onto the Forest Drive, which is open to vehicles too. It runs parallel to Whitespout Lane and you'll later catch a glimpse of little Loch Gower and Loch Riecawr through the trees. After passing some forestry buildings you'll come close to a car park near the head of Loch Bradan, but you turn left just beforehand to follow a minor road to Stinchar Bridge, where you'll need to be collected by someone.

* * *

WALK 35: THE AWFUL HAND WALK

Distance: 17 miles (27km).

Start: Caldons Campsite - 397791.

Finish: Stinchar Bridge - 387957.

You can start this hard day's walk from Caldons Campsite and cross the whole of the Range of the Awful Hand to reach Stinchar Bridge. Follow a waymarked trail along the northern side of Loch Trool to reach the Bruce's Stone. Rather than climbing the popular Merrick path, it's worth taking a narrow path over the Fell of Eschoncan and crossing Bennan first. You'd join the popular path over Benyellary and continue to Merrick afterwards. Walk off the hill via the Spear of the Merrick and cross a boggy, rocky gap. The broad, bouldery slopes of Kirriereoch Hill give way to a broad, grassy summit. There's a steep, stony northern face to descend, then a broad, hummocky, lochan-strewn gap to cross before a fairly easy ascent of Tarfessock. After passing the summit you drop down to the Nick of Carclach and climb past odd boulders to reach the broad, grassy summit of Shalloch on Minnoch. Descend northwards from the trig point to cross a broad gap and climb over the moorland hump of

North Top. A vague path leads towards Cairnadloch, but you'll lose it before reaching the minor road below. Once you hit the road, simply follow it into the forest to end the walk at Stinchar Bridge, where you should arrange for someone to meet you.

* * *

WALK 36: THE RHINNS OF KELLS WALK

Distance: 15 miles (24km).
Start: Near Loch Head - 482924.
Finish: Craigencallie - 504781.

Arrange for someone to drop you off near the head of Loch Doon and ask them to collect you later from Craigencallie. You follow the forest road past Loch Head and continue along forest rides to the edge of the forest. Rugged slopes head up to the summit of Corran of Portmark, where the walking gets easier. Follow a fence from the summit of Corran to neighbouring Bow, then continue along the fence to Meaul. There's no guide along the broad crest after Meaul, and only a vague path. Cross a broad gap and climb the grassy, whaleback ridge of Carlin's Cairn. Continue southwards towards the bulky, grassy, flat-topped Corserine. A path will be noticed on the descent and this leads along a hummocky ridge up to Millfire. A wall can be followed over Milldown and Meikle Millyea, then you have to guide yourself over some very rugged terrain to cross Little Millyea and Darrou. The final hump on the ridge is Craigwhannel, from where there's a steep and tiring descent to a junction of forest roads. Take a road across the River Dee and turn left to reach Craigencallie.

* * *

WALK 37: THE MINNIGAFF HILLS WALK

Distance: 14 miles (23km).
Start: Craigencallie - 504781.
Finish: Caldons Campsite - 397791.

This walk starts from Craigencallie and crosses the rugged Minnigaff Hills to end at Caldons Campsite. It starts with an ascent of the bouldery Cairnarroch, then continues along the broad crest of the hills to the summit of Millfore. Head off along a rugged, hummocky ridge to descend to the Loup of Laggan. A steep and rugged climb leads to the summit of Curleywee, followed by a descent to the Nick of Curleywee. A line of old fenceposts can be traced up the rugged ridge to Bennanbrack and across the broad, smooth, grassy slopes of Lamachan Hill. As you cross over the Nick of the Brushy you join a wall and follow this over the two summits on the whaleback ridge of Larg Hill. Continue along the wall to descend to a forest road. Turn right and follow the forest road down to Caldons Campsite.

* * *

WALK 38: THE DUNGEON HILLS WALK

Distance: 17 miles (27km).
Start: Caldons Campsite - 397791.
Finish: Near Loch Head - 482924.

The Dungeon Hills are in the middle of the Galloway Hills and need to be approached from a point well away from the range. The route suggested starts from Caldons Campsite and ends near the head of Loch Doon. Follow the course of the Southern Upland Way along the southern side of Loch Trool, continuing above Glenhead to reach a rugged gap in the hills. Head up the rugged slopes of Craiglee, remembering that this is one of the easiest of the Dungeon Hills and that there is some very rough and rocky terrain ahead. Descend via Dow Loch and head towards Craignaw - which is easier said than done. Pick a careful way down from Craignaw to the Nick of the Dungeon, and climb the granite slopes of Craignairny and Dungeon Hill. The huge, bouldery dome of Mullwharchar is crossed next, followed by more rough country on the ascent of Hoodens Hill. A cairned path leads northwards along the ridge, then you need to look for an exit using paths along forest rides to cross Gala Lane. A forest road leads towards the head of Loch Doon. You'll need plenty of time to complete all of this walk and should arrange to be collected near Loch Doon afterwards.

* * *

WALK 39: THE GRAND TOUR

This walk is a combination of all four of the longer hill walks which have been suggested. In order to complete this walk, which would take up to five days, you'll either have to carry a tent and all your gear, or rely on bothies for overnight shelter. The Grand Tour covers the Range of the Awful Hand, then crosses bleak and boggy country before traversing the Rhinns of Kells. A walk along that range is followed by a crossing of the Minnigaff Hills. You can stock up with food at the campsite shop before heading through the rugged Dungeon Hills in the middle of the Galloway Hills. The total distance of this walk is 74 miles (119km), and you must bear in mind that such an extended backpack is a difficult and energy-sapping undertaking.

* * *

Day 1: Caldons to Tunskeen

Distance: 16 miles (26km).

Start at Caldons Campsite and follow a waymarked trail along the northern side of Loch Trool to reach the Bruce's Stone. Rather than climbing the popular Merrick path, it's worth taking a narrow path over the Fell of Eschoncan and crossing Bennan first. You'd join the popular path over Benyellary and continue to Merrick afterwards. Walk off the hill via the Spear of the Merrick and cross a boggy, rocky gap. The broad, bouldery slopes of Kirriereoch Hill give way to a broad, grassy summit. There's a steep, stony northern face to descend, then a broad, hummocky, lochan-strewn gap to cross before a fairly easy ascent of Tarfessock. After passing the summit you drop down to the Nick of Carclach and climb past odd boulders to reach the broad, grassy summit of Shalloch on Minnoch. Descend northwards, avoiding the rocky ridge of The Cargie, to reach a broad, boggy, hummocky gap. Turn right to follow Craigendoof Burn down to a forest road, then right again to follow the road and a path to the Tunskeen Bothy for the night.

* * *

Day 2: Tunskeen to Backhill of Bush

Distance: 16 miles (26km).

Leave the Tunskeen Bothy and walk eastwards to cross the rugged slopes of Macaterick. Descend carefully, continuing eastwards across tussocky grass to cross Eglin Lane. Climb over the northernmost part of the ridge of Hoodens Hill and use paths along forest rides to cross Gala Lane. A forest road leads towards the head of Loch Doon, where you turn right and follow a forest road and forest rides to the edge of the forest. Rugged slopes head up to the summit of Corran of Portmark, where the walking gets easier. Follow a fence from the summit of Corran to neighbouring Bow, then continue along the fence to Meaul. There's no guide along the broad crest after Meaul, and only a vague path. Cross a broad gap and climb the grassy, whaleback ridge of Carlin's Cairn. Continue southwards towards the bulky, grassy, flat-topped Corserine. If you need shelter for the night then you can descend to the Backhill of Bush Bothy.

* * *

Day 3: Backhill of Bush to White Laggan

Distance: 14 miles (23km).

Climb back onto the Rhinns of Kells to continue the walk by following a path along a hummocky ridge and up to Millfire. A wall can be followed over Milldown and Meikle Millyea, then you have to guide yourself over some very rugged terrain to cross Little Millyea and Darrou. The final hump on the ridge is Craigwhannel, from where there's a steep and tiring descent to a junction of forest roads. Take a road across the River Dee and turn left to reach Craigencallie. Climb up the bouldery Cairnarroch, then continue along the broad crest of the hills to the summit of Millfore. Head off along a rugged, hummocky ridge to descend to the Loup of Laggan. You can descend from this gap along an old, boggy road to reach the White Laggan Bothy for the night.

* * *

Day 4: White Laggan to Caldons

Distance: 11 miles (17km).

Leave the White Laggan Bothy and walk back up to the Loup of Laggan. A steep and rugged climb leads to the summit of Curleywee, followed by a descent to the Nick of Curleywee. A line of old fenceposts can be traced up the rugged ridge to Bennanbrack and across the broad, smooth, grassy slopes of Lamachan Hill. As you cross over the Nick of the Brushy you join a wall and follow this over the two summits on the whaleback ridge of Larg Hill. Continue along the wall to descend to a forest road. Turn right and follow the forest road down to Caldons Campsite, where you can replenish your food supplies at the campsite shop.

* * *

Day 5: Caldons to Loch Doon

Distance: 17 miles (27km).

You have now completed a major circuit of the hills, but you can continue into the heart of the region by walking through the rocky Dungeon Hills. Start by following the course of the Southern Upland Way along the southern side of Loch Trool, continuing above Glenhead to reach a rugged gap in the hills. Head up the rugged slopes of Craiglee, remembering that this is one of the easiest of the Dungeon Hills and that there is some very rough and rocky terrain ahead. Descend via Dow Loch and head towards Craignaw - which is easier said than done. Pick a careful way down from Craignaw to the Nick of the Dungeon, and climb the granite slopes of Craignairny and Dungeon Hill. The huge, bouldery dome of Mullwharchar is crossed next, followed by more rough country on the ascent of Hoodens Hill. A cairned path leads northwards along the ridge, then you need to look for an exit using paths along forest rides to cross Gala Lane. A forest road leads towards the head of Loch Doon. You can either arrange to be collected at this point, or consider following the low-level Forest Walk back to Caldons Campsite.

* * *

WALK 40: THE SOUTHERN UPLAND WAY

The Southern Upland Way has been mentioned in a number of places in this guidebook. It is Scotland's longest waymarked trail and runs for 212 miles (341km) from Portpatrick to Cockburnspath - coast to coast across the Southern Uplands. Walkers who want to complete the distance need to use two publications. One is a copy of *The Southern Upland Way*, by Roger Smith, published by HMSO; and the other is an annually revised leaflet listing all the available services along the way. If you were to walk the route relying solely on B&B or hostel accommodation, then your schedule would include some very long days. Many walkers carry a tent and also stay indoors using the basic accommodation offered by bothies at intervals along the way. A suggested schedule is given here, outlining the route and pointing out accommodation options along the way.

* * *

Day 1: Portpatrick to New Luce

Distance: 23 miles (37km)

Portpatrick has a small harbour and used to have a major link with Ireland, but most freight goes via Stranraer these days. Its poky streets are worthy walking if you stay overnight. An easy cliff path leaves the village, becoming more difficult towards Black Head. Turn inland at Black Head and walk on roads to Knock and Maize. Low moors are crossed and a reservoir is seen, then you have a decision to make. If you started early in the day, then you can keep walking, but if you started late, then you could aim for Stranraer for the night and continue to New Luce in the morning. Minor roads and tracks cross flat ground to reach Castle Kennedy, which has a shop and hotel. Ornamental gardens are passed by White Loch, then a road walk leads to the splendid farmhouse of Chlenry. The Southern Upland Way goes through a forest and across a railway, then uses a suspension footbridge to cross the Water of Luce. New Luce is a little off-route but it has accommodation and a shop.

* * *

Day 2: New Luce to Bargrennan

Distance: 17 miles (27km)

A farm track near New Luce climbs to Kilhern, then drops down to a waterfall near Barnshangan. A road climbs past a farm and a track continues over extensive enclosed moorlands. Forest covers the moors around Craigairie Fell, and the route follows an assortment of paths and tracks. Standing stones are passed in a clearing at Laggangarn, where there is a new shelter. The route wanders down to the solitary farmstead of Derry, which has snacks and accommodation. Follow the access road away from Derry, passing through more forest. A minor road crosses rivers and passes through an open area before another road leads to Knowe. The route goes through forest again, then follows a road passing Glenruther. The road is left briefly in favour of a path over Glenvernoch Fell, then at Garchew the route cuts across fields to descend to Bargrennan. The tiny village has accommodation.

* * *

Day 3: Bargrennan to Dalry

Distance: 24 miles (39km)

This is a long, hard day's walk through the hills which are covered by the rest of this guidebook. The Southern Upland Way leaves Bargrennan and climbs over the forested Rig of the Cairn. The Water of Trool is followed to Caldons Campsite, where a small shop can be found. The path leaving Caldons is muddy in places and passes the Steps of Trool, where Robert the Bruce ambushed an English force. The path becomes easier as it descends, then it climbs above Glenhead Burn. Views from a track look across Loch Dee and take in the Rhinns of Kells. The White Laggan Bothy is just off-route if shelter is required. Follow forest tracks across the Black Water of Dee and continue around Clatteringshaws Loch. Tracks and paths lead out of the forest and across Shield Rig before descending to a road beside Garroch Burn. Although the walk onwards to Dalry is fairly easy, it can seem tough when you are tired. One of the B&Bs in Dalry operates a *Southern Upland Way Vehicle Support* - though this must be arranged in advance. The road follows Garroch Burn downstream, then you cross the Water of Ken to reach Dalry. The village offers a full range of facilities.

* * *

Day 4: Dalry to Sanquhar

Distance: 27 miles (43km)

This is another long day's walk, though there are ways to split the distance over two days. If you are using the *Southern Upland Way Vehicle Support,* then you can break at Stroanpatrick and return to Dalry for another night. You would then continue from Stroanpatrick. All other accommodation is well off-route, such as Kendoon Youth Hostel and a couple of solitary B&Bs. The Chalk Memorial Bothy, however, is on the route at Polskeoch. You should consider all your options before leaving Dalry, then use paths and tracks to pass Ardoch and cross Earlstoun Burn. A road leads to Butterhole Bridge, before the route crosses Culmark Hill. Another road is crossed at Stroanpatrick, then the route leads over the recently forested Manquhill Hill. Benbrack is crossed at 580m, and if you stay near the forest you'll also cross Black Hill. Enter the forest to pass Allan's Cairn, from where a lengthy descent leads to the Chalk Memorial at Polskeoch. A minor road runs down the glen and passes isolated farms. Leave the road at Polgown, follow a path over Cloud Hill before descending to Sanquhar. The town has good facilities and the oldest post office in Britain.

* * *

Day 5: Sanquhar to Wanlockhead

Distance: 8 miles (13km)

This is a short day, so that you can either recover after yesterday's walk, or catch up if you broke early at Polskeoch. An easy climb up from Sanquhar leads into the hills, then there is a choice of routes in the forest at Cogshead. One route follows forest paths and tracks and is available all year. The other route is restricted during lambing time and the grouse-shooting season. Whichever route you choose to reach Wanlockhead, aim to spend as much time as you can exploring a vast open-air museum - which means even more walking! Wanlockhead is the highest village in Scotland and has a fair number of facilities.

* * *

Day 6: Wanlockhead to Beattock

Distance: 20 miles (32km)

Leave Wanlockhead and climb to the 725m summit of Lowther Hill - the highest point on the Southern Upland Way. A road also runs to this height to reach masts and "radomes". Walk downhill, enjoying views ahead in clear weather. Fences and walls guide you across Cold Moss, Comb Head and Laght Hill, before you drop down to a road at Over Fingland. After crossing Potrail Water a forest track leads to a road near Daer Reservoir. A climb up Sweetshaw Brae leads onto Hods Hill, then the route wanders along the crest of the hills. A descent leads into forest and crosses a stream close to the Brattleburn Bothy. The route runs over Craig Hill, the crosses a pasture to reach Garpol Water. More forest is encountered over Neath Hill before a road leads down to Beattock. A good range of facilities are available and the shop should be visited as supplies could be hard to obtain for a few days.

* * *

Day 7: Beattock to Tibbie Shiels Inn

Distance: 21 miles (34km)

Beyond Beattock the route crosses Annandale and follows Moffat Water. A forest track climbs high alongside Cornal Burn, then the route crosses a rugged gap at Ettrick Head around 530m. another forest track runs past the isolated bothy at Over Phawhope. A road runs through the Ettrick Valley and you may find a lodging, or snacks at a farmhouse. Scabcleuch Burn leads back into the hills and the route reaches 450m on a gap. A valley is crossed at Riskinhope Hope, then from a forest on Earl's Hill a track leads down to Tibbie Shiels Inn. The inn offers food and accommodation, while a cafe and shop can be found by the Loch of the Lowes. A statue of James Hogg also overlooks the loch.

* * *

Day 8: Tibbie Shiels Inn to Broadmeadows

Distance: 22 miles (35km)

A path and forest track lead around the shore of St Mary's Loch, then the route passes Dryhope and Blackhouse. As it climbs into the hills, the Southern Upland Way touches 476m on Deuchar Law and 461m on Blake Muir. A descent leads to Kirkhope, then a road is followed to Traquair. The town of Innerleithen is off-route if you need to visit the shops. There are no more shops until Galashiels is reached. A track climbs above Traquair and passes through forest on its way to the Cheese Well on Minch Moor. The route follows a moorland crest, crossing Hare Law and reaching 524m on Bovery Law. You need to decide at that point whether to press onwards to Galashiels, or drop down to the Youth Hostel at Broadmeadows for the night.

* * *

Day 9: Broadmeadows to Lauder

Distance: 21 miles (34km)

Hostellers from Broadmeadows need to climb up to the tall cairns at 464m on the Three Brethren. A descent through forest can be muddy. After crossing the Tweed near the village of Yair, tracks and paths lead over Hog Hill to Galashiels. The route stays above the town, but there are shops down in town if required. The Tweed is reached again near Abbotsford - once home of Sir Walter Scott. An old railway trackbed and riverside path lead to Melrose, which has a full range of facilities and a splendid ruined abbey. Leave town by crossing a fine suspension footbridge over the Tweed, then follow good tracks above Wester and Easter Housebyres. The route is quite direct over Mosshouses Moor and included a stretch of minor road. A path later runs down to Lauder Burn and the little town of Lauder is soon reached. Accommodation and shops are available, and you should note that such facilities become very sparse beyond the town.

* * *

Day 10: Lauder to Longformacus

Distance: 15 miles (24km)

Leaving Lauder, the Southern Upland Way crosses over the Lammermuir Hills and you need to keep a careful eye on the route. After crossing Lauder Water, forest tracks and farm tracks lead gradually uphill. There are rivers to cross at Snawdon Burn and Blythe Water. After crossing Scoured Rig and passing a small forest a track leads down to a remote building at Braidshawrig. A fine track leads over the moors, gradually climbing towards two cairns on Twin Law at 447m. One of the cairns has a visitors book! Descending from Twin Law, the route leads to Water Watch Reservoir, from where a road continues down into Longformacus. The village has no shops and only one B&B. The next lodging is the Youth Hostel at Abbey St Bathans.

* * *

Day 11: Longformacus to Cockburnspath

Distance: 17 miles (27km)

Follow a road away from Longformacus, then the route leads up into Moor Plantation and Owl Wood before descending through Lodge Wood. The Southern Upland Way passes above Ellemford Bridge, then later runs down through Roughside Wood to follow Whiteadder Water downstream. Abbey St Bathans has a Youth Hostel and a tearoom in a charming estate setting. The remainder of the Southern Upland Way is quite easy, but there are some uphills and downhills. The route heads for the hilltop settlement of Blackburn, then a quiet road runs down to a very busy road. After crossing a railway the route stays high above a wooded valley before heading for the sea. A cliff path is followed which overlooks a tiny harbour. The Southern Upland Way turns inland to end in the village of Cockburnspath, where a fair number of facilities are available - a long way from the Galloway Hills!

LISTING OF CICERONE GUIDES

NORTHERN ENGLAND LONG DISTANCE TRAILS

- THE DALES WAY
- THE ISLE OF MAN COASTAL PATH
- THE PENNINE WAY
- THE ALTERNATIVE COAST TO COAST
- NORTHERN COAST-TO-COAST WALK
- THE RELATIVE HILLS OF BRITAIN
- MOUNTAINS ENGLAND & WALES
  VOL 1 WALES
  VOL 2 ENGLAND

CYCLING

- BORDER COUNTRY BIKE ROUTES
- THE CHESHIRE CYCLE WAY
- THE CUMBRIA CYCLE WAY
- THE DANUBE CYCLE WAY
- LANDS END TO JOHN O'GROATS CYCLE GUIDE
- ON THE RUFFSTUFF - 84 BIKE RIDES IN NORTH ENGLAND
- RURAL RIDES NO.1 WEST SURREY
- RURAL RIDES NO.1 EAST SURREY
- SOUTH LAKELAND CYCLE RIDES
- THE WAY OF ST JAMES LE PUY TO SANTIAGO - CYCLIST'S

LAKE DISTRICT AND MORECAMBE BAY

- CONISTON COPPER MINES
- CUMBRIA WAY & ALLERDALE RAMBLE
- THE CHRONICLES OF MILNTHORPE
- THE EDEN WAY
- FROM FELL AND FIELD
- KENDAL - A SOCIAL HISTORY
- A LAKE DISTRICT ANGLER'S GUIDE
- LAKELAND TOWNS
- LAKELAND VILLAGES
- LAKELAND PANORAMAS
- THE LOST RESORT?
- SCRAMBLES IN THE LAKE DISTRICT
- MORE SCRAMBLES IN THE LAKE DISTRICT
- SHORT WALKS IN LAKELAND
  BOOK 1: SOUTH
  BOOK 2: NORTH
  BOOK 3: WEST
- ROCKY RAMBLER'S WILD WALKS
- RAIN OR SHINE
- ROADS AND TRACKS OF THE LAKE DISTRICT
- THE TARNS OF LAKELAND VOL 1: WEST
- THE TARNS OF LAKELAND VOL 2: EAST
- WALKING ROUND THE LAKES
- WALKS SILVERDALE/ARNSIDE
- WINTER CLIMBS IN LAKE DISTRICT

NORTH-WEST ENGLAND

- WALKING IN CHESHIRE
- FAMILY WALKS IN FOREST OF BOWLAND
- WALKING IN THE FOREST OF BOWLAND
- LANCASTER CANAL WALKS
- WALKER'S GUIDE TO LANCASTER CANAL
- CANAL WALKS VOL 1: NORTH
- WALKS FROM THE LEEDS-LIVERPOOL CANAL
- THE RIBBLE WAY
- WALKS IN RIBBLE COUNTRY
- WALKING IN LANCASHIRE
- WALKS ON THE WEST PENNINE MOORS
- WALKS IN LANCASHIRE WITCH COUNTRY
- HADRIAN'S WALL
  VOL 1 : THE WALL WALK
  VOL 2 : WALL COUNTRY WALKS

NORTH-EAST ENGLAND

- NORTH YORKS MOORS
- THE REIVER'S WAY
- THE TEESDALE WAY
- WALKING IN COUNTY DURHAM
- WALKING IN THE NORTH PENNINES
- WALKING IN NORTHUMBERLAND
- WALKING IN THE WOLDS
- WALKS IN THE NORTH YORK MOORS BOOKS 1 AND 2
- WALKS IN THE YORKSHIRE DALES BOOKS 1,2 AND 3
- WALKS IN DALES COUNTRY
- WATERFALL WALKS - TEESDALE & HIGH PENNINES
- THE YORKSHIRE DALES
- YORKSHIRE DALES ANGLER'S GUIDE

THE PEAK DISTRICT

- STAR FAMILY WALKS PEAK DISTRICT/STH YORKS
- HIGH PEAK WALKS
- WEEKEND WALKS IN THE PEAK DISTRICT
- WHITE PEAK WALKS
  VOL.1 NORTHERN DALES
  VOL.2 SOUTHERN DALES
- WHITE PEAK WAY
- WALKING IN PEAKLAND
- WALKING IN SHERWOOD FOREST
- WALKING IN STAFFORDSHIRE
- THE VIKING WAY

WALES AND WELSH BORDERS

- ANGLESEY COAST WALKS
- ASCENT OF SNOWDON
- THE BRECON BEACONS
- CLWYD ROCK
- HEREFORD & THE WYE VALLEY
- HILLWALKING IN SNOWDONIA
- HILLWALKING IN WALES VOL.1
- HILLWALKING IN WALES VOL.2
- LLEYN PENINSULA COASTAL PATH
- WALKING OFFA'S DYKE PATH
- THE PEMBROKESHIRE COASTAL PATH
- THE RIDGES OF SNOWDONIA
- SARN HELEN
- SCRAMBLES IN SNOWDONIA
- SEVERN WALKS
- THE SHROPSHIRE HILLS
- THE SHROPSHIRE WAY
- SPIRIT PATHS OF WALES
- WALKING DOWN THE WYE
- A WELSH COAST TO COAST WALK
- WELSH WINTER CLIMBS

THE MIDLANDS

- CANAL WALKS VOL 2: MIDLANDS
- THE COTSWOLD WAY
- COTSWOLD WALKS
  BOOK 1: NORTH
  BOOK 2: CENTRAL
  BOOK 3: SOUTH
- THE GRAND UNION CANAL WALK
- HEART OF ENGLAND WALKS
- WALKING IN OXFORDSHIRE
- WALKING IN WARWICKSHIRE
- WALKING IN WORCESTERSHIRE
- WEST MIDLANDS ROCK

SOUTH AND SOUTH-WEST ENGLAND

- WALKING IN BEDFORDSHIRE
- WALKING IN BUCKINGHAMSHIRE
- CHANNEL ISLAND WALKS
- CORNISH ROCK
- WALKING IN CORNWALL
- WALKING IN THE CHILTERNS
- WALKING ON DARTMOOR
- WALKING IN DEVON
- WALKING IN DORSET
- CANAL WALKS VOL 3: SOUTH
- EXMOOR & THE QUANTOCKS
- THE GREATER RIDGEWAY
- WALKING IN HAMPSHIRE
- THE ISLE OF WIGHT
- THE KENNET & AVON WALK
- THE LEA VALLEY WALK
- LONDON THEME WALKS
- THE NORTH DOWNS WAY
- THE SOUTH DOWNS WAY
- THE ISLES OF SCILLY
- THE SOUTHERN COAST TO COAST
- SOUTH WEST WAY
  VOL.1 MINEH'D TO PENZ.
  VOL.2 PENZ. TO POOLE
- WALKING IN SOMERSET
- WALKING IN SUSSEX
- THE THAMES PATH
- TWO MOORS WAY
- WALKS IN KENT BOOK 1
- WALKS IN KENT BOOK 2
- THE WEALDWAY & VANGUARD WAY

SCOTLAND

- WALKING IN THE ISLE OF ARRAN
- THE BORDER COUNTRY A WALKERS GUIDE
- BORDER COUNTRY CYCLE ROUTES

- BORDER PUBS & INNS - A WALKERS' GUIDE
- CAIRNGORMS, WINTER CLIMBS 5TH EDITION
- CENTRAL HIGHLANDS 6 LONG DISTANCE WALKS
- WALKING THE GALLOWAY HILLS
- WALKING IN THE HEBRIDES
- NORTH TO THE CAPE
- THE ISLAND OF RHUM
- THE ISLE OF SKYE A WALKER'S GUIDE
- WALKS IN THE LAMMERMUIRS
- WALKING IN THE LOWTHER HILLS
- THE SCOTTISH GLENS SERIES
  1 - CAIRNGORM GLENS
  2 - ATHOLL GLENS
  3 - GLENS OF RANNOCH
  4 - GLENS OF TROSSACH
  5 - GLENS OF ARGYLL
  6 - THE GREAT GLEN
  7 - THE ANGUS GLENS
  8 - KNOYDART TO MORVERN
  9 - THE GLENS OF ROSS-SHIRE
- SCOTTISH RAILWAY WALKS
- SCRAMBLES IN LOCHABER
- SCRAMBLES IN SKYE
- SKI TOURING IN SCOTLAND
- THE SPEYSIDE WAY
- TORRIDON - A WALKER'S GUIDE
- WALKS FROM THE WEST HIGHLAND RAILWAY
- THE WEST HIGHLAND WAY
- WINTER CLIMBS NEVIS & GLENCOE

IRELAND

- IRISH COASTAL WALKS
- THE IRISH COAST TO COAST
- THE MOUNTAINS OF IRELAND

WALKING AND TREKKING IN THE ALPS

- WALKING IN THE ALPS
- 100 HUT WALKS IN THE ALPS
- CHAMONIX TO ZERMATT
- GRAND TOUR OF MONTE ROSA VOL. 1 AND VOL. 2
- TOUR OF MONT BLANC

FRANCE, BELGIUM AND LUXEMBOURG

- WALKING IN THE ARDENNES
- ROCK CLIMBS BELGIUM & LUX.
- THE BRITTANY COASTAL PATH
- CHAMONIX - MONT BLANC WALKING GUIDE
- WALKING IN THE CEVENNES
- CORSICAN HIGH LEVEL ROUTE: GR20
- THE ECRINS NATIONAL PARK
- WALKING THE FRENCH ALPS: GR5
- WALKING THE FRENCH GORGES
- FRENCH ROCK
- WALKING IN THE HAUTE SAVOIE
- WALKING IN THE LANGUEDOC
- TOUR OF THE OISANS: GR54
- WALKING IN PROVENCE
- THE PYRENEAN TRAIL: GR10
- THE TOUR OF THE QUEYRAS
- ROBERT LOUIS STEVENSON TRAIL
- WALKING IN TARENTAISE & BEAUFORTAIN ALPS
- ROCK CLIMBS IN THE VERDON
- TOUR OF THE VANOISE
- WALKS IN VOLCANO COUNTRY

FRANCE/SPAIN

- ROCK CLIMBS IN THE PYRENEES
- WALKS & CLIMBS IN THE PYRENEES
- THE WAY OF ST JAMES LE PUY TO SANTIAGO - WALKER'S
- THE WAY OF ST JAMES LE PUY TO SANTIAGO - CYCLIST'S

SPAIN AND PORTUGAL

- WALKING IN THE ALGARVE
- ANDALUSIAN ROCK CLIMBS
- BIRDWATCHING IN MALLORCA
- COSTA BLANCA ROCK
- COSTA BLANCA WALKS VOL 1
- COSTA BLANCA WALKS VOL 2
- WALKING IN MALLORCA
- ROCK CLIMBS IN MAJORCA, IBIZA & TENERIFE
- WALKING IN MADEIRA
- THE MOUNTAINS OF CENTRAL SPAIN
- THE SPANISH PYRENEES GR11 2ND EDITION
- WALKING IN THE SIERRA NEVADA
- WALKS & CLIMBS IN THE PICOS DE EUROPA
- VIA DE LA PLATA

SWITZERLAND

- ALPINE PASS ROUTE, SWITZERLAND
- THE BERNESE ALPS A WALKING GUIDE
- CENTRAL SWITZERLAND
- THE JURA: HIGH ROUTE & SKI TRAVERSES
- WALKING IN TICINO, SWITZERLAND
- THE VALAIS, SWITZERLAND - A WALKING GUIDE

GERMANY, AUSTRIA AND EASTERN EUROPE

- MOUNTAIN WALKING IN AUSTRIA
- WALKING IN THE BAVARIAN ALPS
- WALKING IN THE BLACK FOREST
- THE DANUBE CYCLE WAY
- GERMANY'S ROMANTIC ROAD
- WALKING IN THE HARZ MOUNTAINS
- KING LUDWIG WAY
- KLETTERSTEIG NORTHERN LIMESTONE ALPS
- WALKING THE RIVER RHINE TRAIL
- THE MOUNTAINS OF ROMANIA
- WALKING IN THE SALZKAMMERGUT
- HUT-TO-HUT IN THE STUBAI ALPS
- THE HIGH TATRAS

SCANDANAVIA

- WALKING IN NORWAY
- ST OLAV'S WAY

ITALY AND SLOVENIA

- ALTA VIA - HIGH LEVEL WALKS DOLOMITES
- CENTRAL APENNINES OF ITALY
- WALKING CENTRAL ITALIAN ALPS
- WALKING IN THE DOLOMITES
- SHORTER WALKS IN THE DOLOMITES
- WALKING ITALY'S GRAN PARADISO
- LONG DISTANCE WALKS IN ITALY'S GRAN PARADISO
- ITALIAN ROCK
- WALKS IN THE JULIAN ALPS
- WALKING IN SICILY
- WALKING IN TUSCANY
- VIA FERRATA SCRAMBLES IN THE DOLOMITES

OTHER MEDITERRANEAN COUNTRIES

- THE ATLAS MOUNTAINS
- WALKING IN CYPRUS
- CRETE - THE WHITE MOUNTAINS
- THE MOUNTAINS OF GREECE
- JORDAN - WALKS, TREKS, CAVES ETC.
- THE MOUNTAINS OF TURKEY
- TREKS & CLIMBS WADI RUM JORDAN
- CLIMBS & TREKS IN THE ALA DAG
- WALKING IN PALESTINE

HIMALAYA

- ADVENTURE TREKS IN NEPAL
- ANNAPURNA - A TREKKER'S GUIDE
- EVEREST - A TREKKERS' GUIDE
- GARHWAL & KUMAON - A TREKKER'S GUIDE
- KANGCHENJUNGA - A TREKKER'S GUIDE
- LANGTANG, GOSAINKUND & HELAMBU TREKKERS GUIDE
- MANASLU - A TREKKER'S GUIDE

OTHER COUNTRIES

- MOUNTAIN WALKING IN AFRICA - KENYA
- OZ ROCK – AUSTRALIAN CRAGS
- WALKING IN BRITISH COLUMBIA
- TREKKING IN THE CAUCAUSUS
- GRAND CANYON & AMERICAN SOUTH WEST
- ROCK CLIMBS IN HONG KONG
- ADVENTURE TREKS WEST NORTH AMERICA
- CLASSIC TRAMPS IN NEW ZEALAND

TECHNIQUES AND EDUCATION

- SNOW & ICE TECHNIQUES
- ROPE TECHNIQUES
- THE BOOK OF THE BIVVY
- THE HILLWALKER'S MANUAL
- THE TREKKER'S HANDBOOK
- THE ADVENTURE ALTERNATIVE
- BEYOND ADVENTURE
- FAR HORIZONS - ADVENTURE TRAVEL FOR ALL
- MOUNTAIN WEATHER

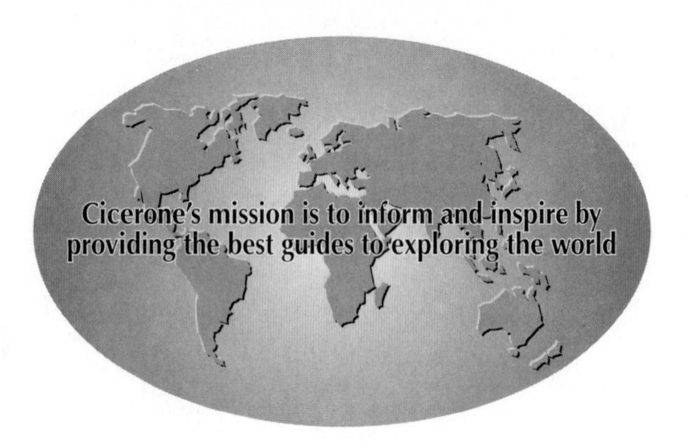

Since its foundation over 30 years ago, Cicerone has specialised in publishing guidebooks and has built a reputation for quality and reliability. It now publishes nearly 300 guides to the major destinations for outdoor enthusiasts, including Europe, UK and the rest of the world.

Written by leading and committed specialists, Cicerone guides are recognised as the most authoritative. They are full of information, maps and illustrations so that the user can plan and complete a successful and safe trip or expedition – be it a long face climb, a walk over Lakeland fells, an alpine traverse, a Himalayan trek or a ramble in the countryside.

With a thorough introduction to assist planning, clear diagrams, maps and colour photographs to illustrate the terrain and route, and accurate and detailed text, Cicerone guides are designed for ease of use and access to the information.

If the facts on the ground change, or there is any aspect of a guide that you think we can improve, we are always delighted to hear from you.

Cicerone Press
2 Police Square Milnthorpe Cumbria LA7 7PY
Tel:01539 562 069 Fax:01539 563 417
e-mail:info@cicerone.co.uk web:www.cicerone.co.uk